USING
ACTIVITIES
in Training and Development

USING ACTIVITIES

in Training and Development

Leslie Rae

KOGAN
PAGE

First published in 1996

Kogan Page Limited
120 Pentonville Road
London N1 9JN

© Leslie Rae, 1996

British Library Cataloguing in Publication Data
A CIP record for this book is available from the British Library.

ISBN 0 7494 1891 5

Typeset by Kogan Page
Printed and bound in Great Britain by Clays Ltd, St Ives plc

Contents

Contents

Preface

Activities, experiential or practical learning events, form a major part of many training programmes today, although this has not always been the case. They offer the learner the opportunity to move from being a passive receiver to an active participant, involved in the learning process. They give the shy, quiet, retiring member, or the one who has a fear of exposing themselves in a group, the chance to be an effective part of the group and make a positive contribution to its success. Activities have a place not only in direct training programmes but also in self-learning, via perhaps an open learning programme; with activity the programme ceases to be merely a 'sit and read this/watch this, and learn' to 'get up now and do it and really learn'.

Activities have their base in the mists of time following the advice accredited to a famous Chinese philosopher:

I listen, I forget
I see, I understand
I do, I remember.

After all, learning is not just about understanding principles, concepts, techniques and approaches, but being able to remember what has been learned and applying it in the working environment.

It must be remembered that activities are not learning itself, merely the first part of active learning, and they must be supported by a variety of other skills – briefing, observing, feedback and so on. Too often the activity alone becomes what is seen as the learning event.

Experiential processes, of course, have their dangers and disadvantages in the same way that other techniques can fail to be effective. A training course can become known as the 'playschool' if too many activities or games are included, just as it could be called the 'classroom' if too much didactic lecturing was the order of the day. If they are used as part of a balanced programme activities can enhance the learning. It is rare for them to reduce the programme time, in fact often the reverse if they are used to full effectiveness. But they can help to use the learning time more effectively and more interestingly, and move it nearer to the world of work (ie doing things) than can sitting listening to a lecture.

PURPOSE OF THE BOOK

The book has simple purposes or objectives; namely to suggest to you the practitioner – whether you are a trainer, instructor, facilitator, training manager, teacher or manager who has a part-time interest or involvement in the process of people's learning – the various forms of activity available to you, along with guidance on how you might use them as effectively as possible.

Many forms of learning programmes have common approaches to the use of activities and the first six chapters describe these in detail. Variations relating to specific types of activities are examined in the later chapters. Common approaches include observing both group and one-to-one activities, reviewing and giving feedback as a result of the observations, planning and designing activities, and the essential pre-activity briefing.

Section two consists of chapters describing the various forms of activities, each chapter including a description of the activity; membership and timing requirements; planning and design; usage - including methods, briefing, observation and reviewing; examples and sources of resources; possible problems and their avoidance; variations. Naturally between many of the different forms of activities there will be common approaches – these will have been dealt with in the early chapters or will have comments only if there are specific variations due to the type of activity. Cross-references will be made so that if the guidance is not repeated in one activity you will know where in the book to obtain the information.

Finally, some practitioners (including those in the educational areas) draw back from practical activities with the view that they are too difficult to use, or the participants will not like them (eg senior managers will think they are childish games), or failure will be catastrophic for the learners, the trainer and the learning programme. My experience has been the reverse of all of these – most activities are fairly simple to run. (If you find one that is too complex, look around; there are many more.) Adults are only big children and few will object to playing a game provided they can see the learning to be achieved from it and how its concepts can be applied at work; certainly there will be failures, but these offer as much, if not more learning than the successes if they are handled in the appropriate way.

Preface

I must thank Dolores Black and Liz Roberts at Kogan Page for their continued support and encouragement in the production of this book and also Jacqueline Twyman of First Impressions who was responsible for correcting my errors and making many valuable suggestions for improvements.

Leslie Rae
November 1995

SECTION ONE

Common Approaches
(to the use of activities)

I
—

Learning Through Experience

Training and development programmes some years ago, and unfortunately still today in many cases, consist of a trainer and/or other expert standing (even rather than sitting) in front of the group of students or trainees and lecturing them. Even the choice of words 'students' and 'trainees' is an indication of the educative type of approach, suggesting that they were there to be taught – whether they wanted or needed to be there. Many of the participants were directed to attend the course and many resented this direction. Attitudes such as this represented the basic recipe for learning not to take place, or to be minimal. 'You can take a horse to water, but you can't make it drink'!

Another cause of minimal learning was that of the trainer, ignoring the enforced attendance, conducting the sessions as lectures in the traditional sense of the word. These are usually straight talks in which the speakers give the audience the benefit of their knowledge on the assumption that the students would listen intently, understand everything, and consequently learn. Many training courses were merely processions of events of this nature, rarely conducted under supportive conditions.

We are not surprised that little learning took place under such conditions. Much *superficial* learning appeared to take place but, unless there were other motivational factors or pressures, little real learning and consequent essential implementation was evident. Realization of this relative failure did not come in one blinding flash of insight, rather it took a while and happened irregularly in both time and location. In fact in many places and with many 'trainers' or their seniors this attitude still exists on the basis that 'they are there to learn, so learn they will.'

However, many researchers and practitioners felt that there must be a more effective way of ensuring that essential messages were not only transmitted, but also received in every sense. The simplest modification from the straight lecture must have appeared at an early stage in a trainer's self-questioning as to whether the students were learning. The 'simplest' because the obvious way to do this is to pose the question or questions to the listeners that will determine the extent to which they have learned. Even a simple, though not always too effective in this form, 'Did you understand that?' would be better than assuming understanding. Even more productive would be the posing of more open questions to seek more extended responses which would suggest the extent of the learning. In this way we progressed from a talk-only situation to a limited form of active involvement, albeit by enforced questioning.

The next stage is one that may be forced on speakers who behave in this manner. Some individuals may be sufficiently motivated to want answers to queries at the time these arise and not to have to wait until the end of the talk when they might be invited to ask questions. They may interrupt the speaker, forcing the speaker to make the decision whether to delay a response until the end of the session (dangerous) or respond immediately (also dangerous). The danger in the first case is that failure to answer immediately may suggest that the speaker:

- does not know the answer;
- cannot be bothered to answer at that stage;
- does not want to answer at that point;
- does not want to take the risk of breaking the thread of the discourse.

Whichever assumption questioners might make as a result of the non-answer, they may reject the remainder of the talk by not listening or simply disagreeing with everything the speaker is saying.

In the second case, if the questions are answered immediately, although the questioner is satisfied and a good relationship is developed, the dangers relate to the speaker who may be hindered from completing all the session's intended material. This may be particularly the case if a number of questions are asked and some supplementary questions or discussion results.

These are real concerns for many trainers and other presenters and the resulting strategy may have to depend on:

- the time available and its flexibility;
- the relationship between the speaker and the audience; and above all
- the speaker's flexibility in presenting the material.

These limited levels of participation and activity may be insufficient to satisfy many learners, particularly at the present time when few course attenders are willing to sit passively for long periods and be expected to learn. The trend over recent years, prompted by a greater understanding of the way people learn, has been for a greater degree of learner active participation in the process and in many cases learner control of the situation – or at least control of *how* a situation might be resolved. This has been the era of the increasing introduction of some form of learner activity through such events as games, exercises, case studies, simulations and other forms of experiential experiences. I tend to describe all these forms of experiences as 'activities'.

EXPERIENTIAL LEARNING

As stated above, most of the progress towards a more participative and experiential approach has resulted from a better understanding of the learning processes, particularly of adults. The simple statement about this is that people learn in different ways, often for different reasons, and effective training and development must recognize these differences and adjust accordingly – as far as is possible.

Experiential learning is frequently expressed in a model known as *The Experiential Learning Cycle*. Although awareness of this principle goes back to, at least, the Greek philosophers, a greater awareness was developed in the 1960s and 1970s, particularly by David Kolb (Kolb *et al.*, 1974) – as a result it is frequently referred to as Kolb's Learning Cycle. Figure 1.1 is a graphical representation of this model in which an individual's learning is seen as beginning with them experiencing something – an action, a feeling and so on. In order to learn from this *experience* it is necessary to do more than live the experience, as so many of us tend to do. The experience should be reflected on in terms of what happened, when certain things happened, who made them happen, what resulted from these actions etc. From this *reflection* you can then start to make conclusions about the experience – what was good and bad about it and why, what worked and what didn't (and why). As a result of *concluding* in this way and identifying what you have learned, you can make plans about how you might behave in a future situation of this nature and certainly what you intend to do with the learning. My experience is that when people undergo a potential learning situation, of the three subsequent possible approaches, the *planning* consideration is the one most likely to be omitted.

5

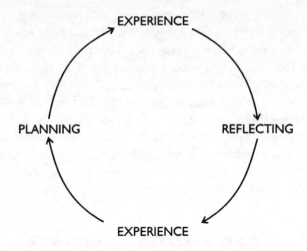

Figure 1.1 *The experiential learning cycle*

Some people consider that the model is too simplistic, giving the impression that all learning must commence with an experience and is a simple progressive cycle from experience round to planning. I have found that in practice the learning does not follow the cycle in a neat progression; frequently learning commences at a different point in the cycle; and, although the cycle describes effective learning, a large number of people do not take advantage of all the stages, principally because most people have different approaches or preferences towards learning and doing. My experience is that although learning can begin with an incident itself, and the learning stages can follow from that event, much commences at an earlier stage. Figure 1.2 suggests a model that describes an alternative approach.

In this alternative experiential learning model the process begins with an identification that you should learn or that there is a potential learning situation existing. This need or situation is then considered in a reflective stage before considering what action can be taken – this consideration is then agreed either with yourself or a third party. Kolb's model then suggests experiencing, reflecting on the experience and concluding from this – this is the central sector of the Figure 1.2 model. It is often then necessary to reconsider the position and approach as a result of errors and omissions in the original path before laying plans for a repetition of the experience, trying a new experience to extend the learning or implementing the learning. The various stages can, therefore, be visited and revisited within a single learning experience before final learning is achieved.

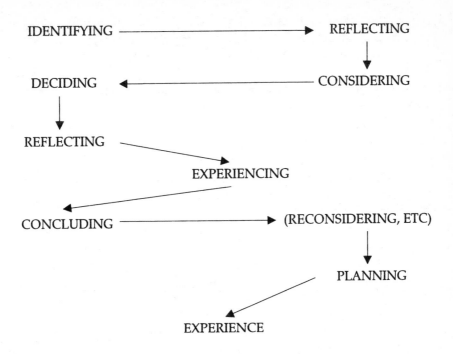

Figure 1.2 *An alternative learning model*

THE HONEY/MUMFORD LEARNING PREFERENCES

Whereabouts in the learning cycle you commence, or to what extent the desirable complete model is used depends, without internal discipline, on your own preferences for learning. Kolb's research which produced his Learning Style Inventory (a development from the Learning Cycle) was carried out in the United States. Somewhat similar studies were conducted in the United Kingdom by Peter Honey and Alan Mumford. However, these two management development consultants and psychologists followed a much more pragmatic path than that of Kolb and the result, the Learning Style Questionnaire, is a more practical instrument for general and training use.

The Honey/Mumford approach is also based on the classical Learning Cycle which, like Kolb's, represents the ideal, fully effective approach to learning. The concept of their model, however starts with the learner doing something, experiencing something, feeling something – an incident – whether it be factual, practical or emotional. Following the experience, learning is reinforced by a period of reflection, during

7

which the learner reflects on what has been observed during and what can be recalled about the experience – *what* in fact happened, *how* it happened, *who* did it, *what* the result was and so on – all the observable incidents which can be stored as factual, detailed information. This activity requires the learner to stop any other or furthering action in order to 'catalogue' the reflections.

In the third stage the data collected is analyzed in terms of the reasons for what happened, the reasons behind the incidence, alternative ways in which the experience might have taken place, an identification of the most effective option, and many other theoretical considerations based on what was done and what was seen to be done. This is the stage of the theorist or conceptualizer.

But conceptualization has to be translated into action if it is to have any worth. This takes place in the fourth stage, the stage when the pragmatist becomes supreme. The watchword of this person is 'If it isn't practical, then it isn't worth anything'. This is the area and the time when the historical considerations are translated into future, practical action by people who care about practicalities.

The cycle then returns to the experience, which may be a repeat of the original experience incorporating the lessons learned in the previous stages. The cycle recommences, hopefully with a shorter lifetime, the lessons learned on the first occasion producing a fully effective event.

LEARNING PREFERENCES

The learner progressing through these stages has learned something at all stages to the extent that an effective function can be performed. This, of course, is the ideal. But in practice most people have a preference for one or more of these learning stages, and if these singular preferences are strong and overpowering problems of complete learning exist.

For example, a learner who becomes 'locked-in' on the active, doing stage is less likely to stop to reflect (or even to consider and reflect before starting) or analyze, and consequently will repeat the original mistakes or even make new ones. The reflector who is so enamoured with considering what has happened will let life pass by with others making decisions, taking action and so on. The locked-in theorist will become so interested in the convolutions of the internal intricacies that nothing will be done. The pragmatist at the end of the cycle might destroy or ignore all that has preceded because if it is not a practical event it must be of no value or interest.

Naturally, not everybody has only one preference. The ideal must be to have a balance of all stage preferences, but in practice most people have one or two strong preferences with the others either weak or just appearing.

APPLICATION TO LEARNING

The models and concepts of learning are not merely interesting theories, but have a direct practical application to our training and development activities. A balanced learning programme *must* contain elements that will satisfy all the learners with their different approaches and preferences and not just the ones that appeal to the trainers. A balanced programme of this nature will include some input of new material with time for the reflectors and theorists to consider this; the activists must be motivated by practical activities, but again must be encouraged to reflect and consider/conclude. Finally, the pragmatic nature of whatever is presented must be made clear for the pragmatists who will be interested only in something that they can implement without difficulty.

All these preference requirements must therefore insist on the inclusion of practical activities, activities which will give all the preference types the opportunity to practise their preferences, and be encouraged to follow the complete, effective learning cycle.

Inclusion of practical, experiential activities lifts the learning programme from the passive, teaching programme described at the beginning of this chapter to an active, interesting, participative event giving all the opportunity not only to learn, but also extend their learning capabilities.

THE ACTIVITY CYCLE

Although, as you will see later in this book, many of the different types of activities require different approaches, there is a common format to their application. The sections dealing with each of these activities will follow this format, although obviously in many cases repetition will be unnecessary. For this format, following the material earlier in this chapter, I should like to present a cycle which I entitle 'The Activity Cycle', shown in Figure 1.3.

Decision-making at the start of the cycle is common to every activity included in a learning programme: During the programme design and planning stage you must make the decisions about whether and to what extent experiential activities are possible and desirable for the particular programme, and where in the programme they are to be included. The choice will naturally depend to a major extent on the type of event and the relevant type of activity, among which are:

- group activities for problem-solving;
- group activities to develop interactive relationships;
- group activities to demonstrate particular management functions – negotiating, presenting, dealing with conflict;
- one-to-one interview situations over a wide range of people contact.

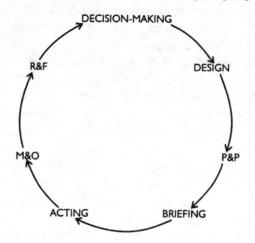

Figure 1.3 *The activity cycle*

There are activities suitable for all these requirements – often there are two problems: finding the most suitable selection in the thousands of published activities and then deciding which one to use. Of course, you may have a selection of your own activities from which to choose: which is going to be the most relevant and effective, the one from your own collection or some other published activity?

The basic criterion for experiential learning must be that wherever possible you should use relevant activities, balancing their number with other types of approach, to ensure not only a full coverage of the subject but also the learning preference satisfaction of your group of learners. Sometimes it is possible to identify strong learning preferences either before the training programme or at the very start – this may give you the opportunity to make a last-minute decision on the number and types of activity to include for that particular learning group. However, your aim must not necessarily be to pander to 'locked-in' preference learners, but to try to extend their learning ranges and capabilities.

Equally you must guard against including too many activities. When experiential learning started to be included in the training pattern some trainers decided that the traditional approach of input sessions was a complete waste of time, and their courses became full of activities. This was carried to the extent that much training suffered from the derogatory label of 'games machine'. A sensible approach to mixed techniques and methods is much more likely to pay dividends that a very biased approach, much in the same way that the locked-in learner loses so many opportunities for real learning.

THE MIXED SESSION

Many activities are used in conjunction with other training approaches, usually an input session of some nature. A typical session might take the form of:

- a brief introduction to the subject by the trainer, including a statement of the objectives;
- an activity related to the session material can be introduced to assess the knowledge and skill level of the learners at this stage in the learning process;
- a short input of new material by the trainer using relevant visual aids and encouraging participation in the form of questioning and discussion;
- at significant points buzz groups might be formed to consider particular items that might arise during the input or discussions;
- an activity can be introduced to practise the learning points of the session;
- the activity is discussed fully, developing the learning points and leading to a summary of the session's learning.

Of course a session of this nature might be more complex than that described above, but the complexity will be principally the inclusion of more discussions, buzz groups and activities. But you must ensure that you are not overloading the session with too much material and too many aspects.

Reference

Kolb, D A, Rubin, I M and McIntyre, J M (1974) *Organizational Psychology – An experiential approach*, Prentice-Hall.

2
—
Initial Action for Activities

Effective activities do not just happen. They take as much planning, design and preparation as any other training event aimed at maximum learning. The attitude of a trainer, deciding during a training programme, without previous consideration 'Let's have an activity now' is often a recipe for failure; but unfortunately it happens all too frequently. Activities are part of the overall planning for a training programme – why have an activity, where will it have most impact and be most effective, what type of activity will be the most suitable and how long will it take/can we afford to spend on it? These are only some of the questions that will have to be answered – following chapters will give detailed guidelines for some of these, the current chapter considering the initial actions necessary in:

- planning;
- resource search or own design;
- preparation for running the activity, both before the training programme and immediately before running the activity;
- briefing participants before the activity.

PLANNING

In the same way that you need to have aims and objectives for your training programme as a whole, so do you need them for the inclusion and practice of activities within the training. Ask yourself:

- Exactly what have I to achieve as a result of this training programme?
- What type of approach am I going to use for the programme?
- What type of learning opportunities am I going to include?
- Specifically, do I want to/need to include practical activities?

- Have I the programme time to include activities?
- Why; how many; what; how; when?

If it has been decided that an activity or activities shall be included, the question above preceded by '◆' must be considered in detail.

Why?

When you are planning your training programme and considering incorporating some forms of activity you must seriously question whether they will improve the learning, or whether you are simply including them because of a personal preference for activities. Activities exclude the need to plan, design and write input sessions – a time-consuming and sometimes very difficult operation – and also having to be a presenter of such sessions – not always an easy choice, even for an experienced presenter.

An activity must be relevant and must contribute something to the event that no other technique will do as effectively. A particular activity may be your personal favourite, and you will naturally try to include it as often as possible – but in spite of your feeling that it is such a good activity, is this the place for it? Or is there another activity, perhaps one that you do not favour as well, that will serve the learning more appropriately? Is an activity relevant? If the learning event is an intensely practical one with lots of demonstrations and practice on, say, the computers involved, it will not be relevant to include an artificial activity when activity is provided by the practical learning itself. In such cases a relevant activity might be a specific task for the learners to perform using the techniques and equipment involved in the learning programme.

The principal reason for using an activity is to consolidate, through practice, learning that has been attained from previous training actions – input sessions, videos and so on – but one of the aspects that can improve a learning situation is to make it into one in which the learning is also fun. A 'heavy' learning programme can often benefit from the infusion of an activity, simply to lighten the atmosphere, when it may be a completely irrelevant, fun activity. This latter type of activity is often called a session shaker – this will be considered in more detail later. There can even be justification for a very selfish use of an activity on the part of the trainer. Long training programmes, with the same group and the same, lone trainer, can become boring for both the learners and the trainer and can require breaks of some nature at intervals – this may be the time for a light session shaker or other activity, the trainer and the learners returning refreshed to the real programme after the lighter activity.

How many?

You will find that this is one of the harder decisions to make. It was mentioned in the previous chapter that as the use of activities was recognized and developed, training programmes were often in danger of becoming playschools because of the excessive use of activities. Unfortunately there is no golden rule to help you to decide this question, other than the trite guideline that your programme should be a balance of different approaches. This balance, however, can be achieved by the use of different types of activities. The input part of the session can be transformed from being a lecture by including at intervals such activities as buzz groups, question and answer periods, discussions on specific parts of the input. Or a video could be included at a relevant point to reinforce or summarize part of the session. After the input, in order to reinforce the learning, an activity can be included, after which a discussion can be held to summarize the learning of the session. This can be looked on as a general recipe for relevant mixing of techniques and approaches within one session.

What is not usually an acceptable format is a very short input followed by a number of activities, one after the other, with the result that the learners become unsettled with so much – particularly the reflector and theorist preference people who want time to reflect on, consider and discuss the preceding activity.

SELECTION OF ACTIVITIES

Once the decision to use activities has been made, the problem of selecting the most appropriate and relevant activity is raised. If we are looking at an already existing programme which includes suitable activities, there is usually little problem. The programme as it stands, if it has been validated as satisfying the objectives of the training and the learners, can continue. But even such successful programmes sometimes need a change as successive groups of learners hear about the programme from previous attenders.

Internally centred activities

One of the accusations often levelled at training programmes that include activities is that the activity is too artificial and too unlike the working environment of the learners. Experience has shown that often more learning is achieved, the activity is more acceptable and the 'poor' learner's shortcomings are less noticeable if the activity is either based on a real work situation or is an actual work situation, preferably one contributed by the learners themselves.

One caveat about internally centred activities is that they must be reviewed at frequent intervals to ensure that they are up to date – corporate policies and strategies do change over time and the credibility of an activity can reduce if these changes have not been taken account of. This caveat is particularly relevant in the case of long-running programmes and also if you, as the new trainer, are taking over an existing programme.

Externally available activities

There will be occasions when an internally centred activity is either not available or not relevant, and the trainer wanting to include new activities must look elsewhere. It must also contain all the learning points you need to include for development, consolidation or testing purposes. Frequently a work-based activity, though apparently relevant, does not include the learning points you seek.

Fortunately the market-place contains a wealth of readily available activities of almost every type that you might require and, though the activity might not relate exactly to the situation for which you require it, most can be modified to make them more relevant. The distaff side of this availability situation is that over the last decade so many collections of activities have been published that, although the activity you want will almost certainly be there, your problem will be finding it! This assumes that you have in your possession all the resource collections.

The first source that you will look at when you require a new activity will be the bank of activities held within your own training organization, if such a bank exists. You may have a collection of your own, or you may be able to tap the facilities of other trainers, within or outside your own organization. Failing this, you can 'invent' your own either by modifying an existing one, or developing it from scratch, building in the learning points that are relevant to your needs.

If these approaches are not possible reference can then be made to the collections mentioned above. As suggested earlier, this is where problems can arise – there are so many collections. The questions that will come to your mind will include:

- In which/whose collection should I look for the appropriate activity?
- I remember seeing an activity that will just fit the bill. In which collection did I see it?

- Have I all/all the best of the collections to which to refer?
- Are there other collections which may contain the activity I am seeking?

The answer to these problems is a universal index of the activities published. But no such index with its desirable listing (description of the activity, objectives, target audience, resources and time required) exists. Something of this nature is available for purchasable, commercially produced games by Chris Elgood (1993), with 300 games being listed.

But the size of the problem becomes evident or becomes much greater if we look for such a description of non-commercial games and collections. Collections of activities of all types are published by Kogan Page, Gower, McGraw-Hill, Longman, BACIE, Pfeiffer etc. When I wrote an article about this problem in 1993, I produced a list of the principal published collections with which I was fairly familiar: the list contained 49 publications containing some 2198 activities (Rae, 1993). Since that date even more collections have been published so the total number is more than 3000.

There is a second major problem with the number of activity collections available. Organizations with virtually bottomless budgets for library, learning or resource centres purchases have no problems – all the published material can be bought (at prices ranging from about £75 to more than £200 per publication). But problems arise if for cost or other reasons a decision has to be made to buy a smaller number than the total. Every activity that has been written must have been an 'original' at some time and many activities of different types must have been produced in this way. Subsequent activities of a similar nature are merely variations on these origins – some very useful variations, some bizarre, some direct copies, others attempts to produce a custom-usable variation. But there is an end to these variations, and so many published are barely disguised copies of the original – which itself was probably plagiarized from another 'original'.

This duplication may not be too much of a problem if you start with no personal nor organization resource library, because it doesn't make too much difference which collection you buy first. The second purchase may create a problem. I have recently read three collections of 'people' role plays, the publications all having different titles but with the activities covering the same situations, with the scenarios modified only slightly. Anyone with an answer to this problem, please write!

When considering a particular collection of activities there is a further factor to take into account. Some collections, like the majority of traditional types of books, have the normal copyright restrictions in which copying without prior permission is forbidden. Others waive all copying restrictions for the purchasers of the collections as long as they use them themselves and do not use them for commercial purposes.

PREPARATORY ACTION

Once you have decided that you are going to use an activity or activities, how many and where in the programme, and have available the appropriate activities, you are ready to take the immediate preparatory action for introducing the activity into the learning event. A personal checklist is a useful instrument, in which you will make notes about the actions you have to take. Such a checklist would include:

- personal familiarity with the activity;
- try out the activity with a group of colleagues;
- produce the necessary briefs and instruction sheets;
- check that you have all the resources available that are required by the activity;
- consider the physical attributes of the participants;
- decide how you are going to select multiple group membership, if relevant;
- check that you have sufficient rooms/space available for multiple groups and that the accommodation is suitable;
- check any safety factors necessary;
- confirm the activity timings;
- prepare your verbal description for the participating groups;
- decide your observation strategy;
- decide what you will do during the activity;
- decide how *you* are going to review the activity;
- make arrangements with participating colleagues to discuss the activity and its use (particularly with a new activity) after it has been used.

Familiarity with the activity

The worst possible scenario is for a trainer to introduce an activity and then be unable to explain clearly to the group what is to happen; to be unable to answer supplementary questions from the participants about the activity; to be unable to carry out an effective briefing at the end of the activity. These inabilities are usually the result of the trainer making inadequate preparation and not being sufficiently familiar with the activity. The latter is frequently caused by a trainer taking over a course with an existing activity, rather than having to selected an activity themselves.

Published activities should have clear and detailed instructions about the activity, how it should be introduced, how it should be carried out, the time required, an indication of the optimum numbers in a group and the numbers of groups and so on. You must make yourself familiar with all these aspects before setting off and asking a learning group to perform the activity – if you fail to prepare, you are preparing to fail.

If you have the opportunity before mounting an activity that is new (to you), it is a valuable experience to persuade a group of your colleagues, trainers or non-trainers, to dummy-run the activity. This will enable you to familiarize yourself with the activity, will show up any problems that might be encountered (with solutions produced by you and your group) and, if it is a new activity that has been custom-made, will check out its validity. You are much more likely to obtain valuable process feedback from a group such as this than rely on either the activity going wrong with the learning group or process feedback from it.

Briefs and instruction sheets

Many activities are too complex and complicated for a simple verbal description to the learning groups to be relied upon. This means that role briefs or group instruction sheets should be constructed or obtained and issued to the participants before the activity. Sufficient time must be allowed for the learners to read and assimilate these briefs, otherwise, quite rightly, they can excuse any failure on insufficient time to prepare. The time will vary with the complexity and length of the brief, so again it is a useful ploy to test out the information with a dummy-run group of colleagues. The material should be tested as if it was the precursor to a 'real' event, under the same conditions and so on.

The preparation of realistic briefs is not easy. They can turn out to be either too long and complex, in which case understanding may be impeded, or they may be too short and snappy, resulting in insufficient information being given to help the participants. The dummy-run should help in this, particularly if the test group is at a similar level to the potential learners. Some briefs are by their very nature short and need to be kept so to allow the learner maximum flexibility. As an example, if you are giving several groups the task of deciding which learning subjects should be included in the following day's programme, the brief might read as Figure 2.1.

Learning Decision

The following topics are available for tomorrow. You have 30 minutes to decide as a group which four topics you would prefer to be included. Be prepared to present your selection to the other groups with reasons for your selection. A final decision will be made in the full group, return to the subgroups being arranged if necessary.

Topics

A .... B ....
C .... D ....
E .... F ....
G .... H ....
I .... J ....

Figure 2.1 *A short brief*

Figure 2.2 shows an even shorter brief – in fact it is so short that the ambiguity of 'analysis' has not been (deliberately) defined.

Car Park Analysis

You have 20 minutes to produce an analysis of the cars in the car park. Write your findings on a sheet of flipchart paper and be prepared to discuss these with the other groups.

Figure 2.2 *An even shorter brief*

Other briefs or instructions will necessarily be longer and more complex – information in a problem-solving case, the detailed role in a role play and so on. But these must be examined closely to ensure that they:

- are not too long and/or complex such that they will confuse the learner;
- are not too short so as to exclude essential information.

Resources

The amount and type of resources needed for an activity will depend on the demands and needs of the activity, but the essential action as far as the trainer is concerned is that all preparations must have been made and the resources all be available before the start of the activity. Your credibility can take a nosedive if you have to admit you have forgotten a resource, or you have to disappear during an activity to obtain a forgotten resource. Some activities will of course require little in the way of resource. Problem-solving activities using, eg Lego bricks, require a complex brief or briefs, a number of solid tables, packs of selected Lego, graph tables, a stop watch, a measure, a recording chart, marker pens, paper and pencils. Ensuring that all the resources required are available and ready for the activity is an essential part of the activity preparation.

Many activities require normal stationery items only, but others, particularly outdoor activities, require more unusual items. You must ensure that you have the authority to obtain them before finally deciding on that activity. Other factors that may be involved with resources include the storage facilities at your training location or elsewhere, or the distance you might have to carry heavy resources from, say, your car to the training location. For example, one resource that I need for an activity that I run at times is a 12 feet long builder's plank!

Most published activities include a list of the resources required, but I would suggest that you (a) make your own checklist to ensure that you have everything and (b) confirm that you do not need any other items that have not been specified – collections sometimes omit resources that are common to all the activities to avoid repetition.

Physical attributes

Possible variations must be considered beforehand or you must be prepared to deal with these at the activity introduction if prior preparation was not possible. Some learners may have a physical disability that would make their participation difficult if the activity involves action that might be a problem for them. This is a particular danger when the disability is not apparent, only emerging when the activity has started. The disability need not be physical only – restrictions of hearing, vision, articulation and so on may not be evident but could restrict the learner in some activities. I am not saying that every activity should be bland, 'safe', undemanding etc as this can be insulting to the learners, but this should be a factor in your preparation and planning.

In summary, although risk should not always be excluded, you must ensure that in your activities there is equality of opportunity and there are no restrictions or problems related to race, colour, beliefs, sex, colour deficiencies, fitness and so on. Careful thought, with a knowledge of both the activity and your learning group during your preparation period, can avoid awkward and embarrassing situations, particularly ones that arise out of nowhere.

Group membership

If it is possible, it is always useful to consider before the event the ways in which your learning group can be divided into subgroups on occasions for activities. Division can be to:

- introduce elements of competition or even conflict;
- ensure the fullest coverage of the topic, using the experience of all members;
- enable practice of intra- and inter-group relationships;
- give practice in presenting material in front of others;
- give as many members as possible the opportunity of playing different roles, including that of the leader;
- encourage the participation of the quiet member who although not contributing during big group events does so in smaller groups.

A number of choices and options are open to you when you are considering the membership of groups in your activities:

- An activity constructed for a single group can often be easily amended to use multi-groups.
- In many cases, if an activity requires, say, four role players in a group, additional people can be included in the group by doubling roles or writing neutral roles.
- Use more observers than you would normally use if you have too many people for completely restricted activities.
- Use a variety of member selection methods for multi-groups.

In the case of the final option shown above, there is a wide variety of methods and choices you can use for group membership selection. Some will obviously depend on the circumstances, some on the type of activity, some on the number of learners you have, some on the specific demands of the activity and some on the use of observers.

Team groups

In events that are concerned with team development it will normally be useful to keep the actual teams together for the whole event, although roles can be switched within the team for each activity. This is particularly the case with the team leader, whose role should be rotated to give other members the chance to be in the shoes of the leader for a time – this will give them the experience of appreciating the problems of the person in that role and their reliance on the other team members.

There can of course be switching of individuals between teams to give the teams practice in the real-life situations of changing membership and the trauma that such changes can often produce.

Other groups

Groups, other than team groups, can be selected before or at the start of the event or activity in a variety of ways:

1. random selection at each activity – dangerous because there might be little mixing as a result;
2. a planned and progressive mixing involving all members of the learning group;
3. separation by choosing points in the group's seating arrangement as cut-offs for the group division;
4. initial mixing, the groups remaining as selected for the whole learning event
5. self-selection by the learners;
6. a homogeneous mix of males and females;
7. a heterogeneous mix of males and females;
8. a hetero- or homogeneous mix of junior and senior members;
9. a hetero- or homogeneous mix of members from different branches of the same organization, or from different organizations;
10. a behavioural analysis approach to selection.

Self-selection

Option 5 above is obviously the most democratic and one which appeals to most, but not all, learning groups, but care must be taken that learning does not suffer because of a non-mixing occurrence. At intervals the groups can of course be asked if they wish to alter their constitutions.

Hetero- and homogeneous mixing

Care must be taken with the decisions between hetero- and homogeneous mixing, even though this may be for the best reasons and may be required by the activity. There can easily be reaction against this type of division and you must explain the reasons for making it.

Option 2 is a frequent, valuable, acceptable to the learners and useful method of mixing, if there are to be a number of activities during an event. A matrix can be produced with the learners entered in simple progression depending on the number of activities, and ensuring that each member has the opportunity to act as leader, member and observer.

Alternatively, a similar matrix can be used but with a more mixed formula involving a more complex mixing of members instead of simple progression.

Behaviour analysis mixing

Option 10 introduces the particular approach of behaviour analysis that is described in Chapter 4. This approach identifies individuals according to their preferences and its practical use as an observational instrument can identify different types of individuals in a number of ways. These varieties of people can be used to mix the learning group in sub-groups, for example:

- separate groups of high, medium and low contributors;
- homogeneous groups of high, medium and low contributors;
- hetero- or homogeneous groups of creative and supportive members;
- hetero- or homogeneous groups of helpful and awkward members.

A 'mixing' caveat must be that you should use mixing for legitimate reasons and not to score or allow the scoring of 'points'. The simplest mixing is often the most effective, and certainly causes you the least problems.

Multiple group accommodation

You might imagine that there is no need to make any comments about accommodation for multiple groups for activities, but it is surprising how often it happens during a learning event that the subgroups are sent to their locations (syndicate or subgroup rooms) only to return saying that the room is in use by someone else. This should not happen, but when it does it is usually the result of deficient preparation.

When you are planning the inclusion of the activity and have decided on the mixing approach, you should then, having determined the number of the subgroups, either ensure that sufficient rooms of an adequate size are reserved (and have the reservations confirmed) or see that there is sufficient space in the main training room for several groups to work almost in isolation. In the latter case you need not be too concerned if you feel that the groups will overhear and contaminate each other's deliberations. If pressure is on the groups to complete the activity and it is sufficiently interesting they will be too busy to be concerned about what the others are doing. You will have to be aware however, of possible problems if one group finishes before the other(s), although this can be useful in increasing the group pressure (if this effect is part of your objectives).

Another frequent failing is for the resources for the syndicate rooms to be forgotten, requiring the learners to break off their activity to come to you to ask for materials (which you might take some time to search for).

These two aspects should certainly form part of your activity checklist used during your preparation period.

Safety

All activities, whether they are physically or mentally active, should be safe. At the mental level no activity should be introduced that is likely to demean or produce loss of face or self-value for any learner. Even the apparently 'toughest' individual can be affected, and there should never be any public attempt made to test this 'toughness' or produce defensive reactions. However, you must be aware that greater risks can be taken in the relatively safe environment of a learning event, particularly if there has been contracting and agreement between the trainer and the learners at the start of the event. This can be in the form of a group or individual contract, when a relationship is formed between the trainer and the learners which includes to what extent both can act or react. This contract should not be assumed, as so often happens, but must be the result of an open discussion.

The group should be brought fully into the construction of this contract so that both they and the trainer own it. The contract should include relationships within the activities that will take place during the event. During an activity statements may be made which should not be divulged elsewhere without consent; comments might be made which others in the group might not like – the contract should include the right of anyone to raise such issues so that the matter might be cleared in a non-aggressive manner. After an activity, in the usual feedback session, the contract should accept that comments should be open and honest, but made in a most effective feedback manner rather than in a sense of negative criticism.

Unless learner members have such contracts relating to what is said and done their contribution to the activities might be less than open and full, and both they and their colleagues will lose something because of this. No one is going to speak if they have the feeling that their contributions are going to be scorned. Although it may seem to be too formal to engage in a contract discussion and agreement at the start of the event, at or about this time is the only period that it can be produced effectively. The dangers of waiting until an incident occurs before it is raised are too horrifying to consider.

Physical safety factors

Apart from outdoor training activities, physical safety factors do not enter excessively into the more normal forms of activity. But this aspect must be considered as some activities do carry some safety aspects – carrying items might be risk factors; the activity in which I use the plank has some risk of people damaging themselves slightly, and so on. If there is any likelihood that the performance of an activity can produce a safety risk, you should ensure that this risk is minimized or avoided altogether, or that the group is informed about it beforehand. Obviously, outdoor training activities fall into a different category and have specific requirements.

Timings

The timing aspects of activities fall into two categories:

- the allocation of time within a learning event; and
- control of the time during an activity.

In the first case, it must be recognized that activities take a considerable amount of time. Time is required for introducing the activity, briefing the participants and the observers, the subgroups moving to their rooms, the activity itself, the review action and any other action resulting from this. This time can vary considerably depending on the type and complexity of the activity. Many activities have an active period of about 30 minutes. This means usually, particularly if several groups are involved, that the review period is about double this. Add the preparation, briefing and movement time, and the time for a short activity of this nature quickly mounts to almost two hours.

When in doubt leave more, rather than less time, otherwise you may be forced into the unfortunate situation of having to rush the participants during the activity itself or have a foreshortened (and consequently ineffective) review and feedback session.

Timing during an activity

There must also be some timing controls during the activity and relating to the activity itself. Many activities are constructed to relate to real-life situations with the many time constraints that exist at work. The learners should be made aware that when they are told that they have 30 minutes for an activity, this means 30 minutes, not 40, and you should ensure that the groups finish at the end of that time, even (or particularly) if they have not completed the task. This lack of completion may in fact be due to their own poor time control – a learning factor of life.

A more effective approach to time allocation and informing the learners about this has been in my experience not to say 'You have 30 minutes' or 'Come back in 30 minutes', but to say 'You have until X o'clock' or 'Finish at X o'clock and return then to the main room'. This should avoid any problems of when the groups should complete and return.

Unless there are administrative reasons why the review period should be contained in the time allocated, this area should have the least time control, particularly if some important learning is emerging from the feedback and discussion. Care should be taken, however, in events with some form of time constraint, that following events are not affected by the use of additional time.

TRAINER DECISIONS

As the trainer introducing the activities you have a number of responsibilities related to the introduction and operation of the activity. Such aspects as the use of observation and reviews are dealt with in detail in later chapters. Two other aspects are:

- how you introduce the activity; and
- what you will do during the activity.

Introducing the activity

Many activities are not stand-alone events but are linked with preceding input sessions, discussion, videos and so on, so there should be some form of bridge between these events and the activity. One school of thought, however, considers that the trainer should say or do nothing other than issue the briefs to the groups and the observers and in effect tell them to 'get on with it.' I feel that this is too stark and can be resented by the learners who may, after all, not relate this new event with what has just gone before. I favour a simple, brief linking statement which can be general advice that an activity is to follow that is related to the preceding material which they will find useful in performing the activity. The learners can then be advised that all they will need (if this is in fact the case) is contained in the briefs and the rooms are available and resourced. You can then withdraw from an active role, although you should still be available to respond to queries and questions.

Additional briefing instruments

You may consider that some learners or learning groups might need a little more than this fairly bare introduction, so issuing a general instruction/briefing sheet can be a helpful addition to the activity brief and role descriptions.

Figure 2.3 suggests the form of a supplementary briefing sheet for the interviewer in a one-to-one role play or the leader in a group activity.

The Interviewer's/Manager's/Group Leader's Briefing List

1. In the role play/group activity in which you are taking part, you will be enacting the role or position of interviewer (manager or supervisor if relevant) or group leader. In the latter case you have full responsibility for your group and authority to take whatever action you feel is justified and relevant within the terms of the activity brief.
2. The approach you should use in the activity should contain as closely as possible the key learning points and skills that have emerged so far in this programme, as they relate to the event.
3. Stick to the activity brief, and unless it is essential to the progress of the activity, do not introduce additional or imaginary material about which the others will know nothing. This is particularly important in the interviews between a manager/supervisor and their staff role plays, unless again it is part of the natural process.
4. Within any constraints of the role allocated, be yourself and react as you would do within the limits of what you *should* do, even if the latter is not your normal (albeit inappropriate) behaviour.
5. Your interviewee/group members are being given a brief in similar terms to this.
6. Please ask now for any further information you feel you require.

Figure 2.3 *A supplementary briefing sheet for the interviewer or group leader*

A supplementary briefing sheet similar to the one shown in Figure 2.3 can be given to the individuals acting as interviewees in a role play or as the group members in a group activity. A suggested format is shown in Figure 2.4

The Interviewee's/Group Members' Briefing Sheet

1. In the role play in which you are taking part you will be enacting the role or position of interviewee/problem-holder.

or

In the group activity in which you are taking part you are a member of that group which has been formed to perform the task described in the task brief, and you are responsible to the leader of the group.

2. The approach you should use in the activity should contain as closely as possible the key learning points and skills that have emerged so far in this programme, as they relate to the event.

3. Stick to the activity brief, and unless it is essential to the progress of the activity, do not introduce additional or imaginary material about which the others will know nothing. This is particularly important in the interview, unless again it is part of the natural process.

4. Within any constraints of the role allocated, be yourself and react as you would do within the limits of what you should do, even if the latter is not your normal (albeit inappropriate) behaviour.

5. Your interviewer/group leader/fellow group members are being given a brief in similar terms to this.

6. Please ask now for any further information you feel you require.

Figure 2.4 *A supplementary briefing sheet for the interviewee or group member*

During the active part of the activity

A major decision that you will have to take is what your personal role will be while the learners are performing the activity. Some options are:

1. disappearing until the allotted time for the return;
2. act as a peripatetic observer, spending a short period with each group, then moving on to the others;
3. staying with one group;
4. not visiting any of the groups but remaining in the main room and letting the groups know you are there in case of major problems.

Option 1 is dangerous because the time during which activities are taking place is completely non-forecastable and where people and places are concerned anything can happen. Better to take option 4 so that the learners know you are available in the last resort.

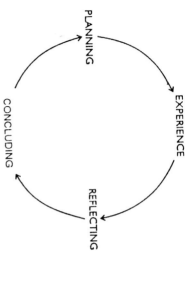

Figure 1.1 *The experiential learning cycle*

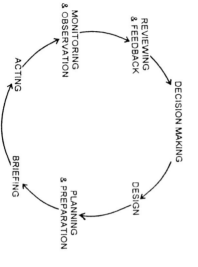

Figure 1.3 *The activity cycle*

ERRATA

Unfortunately errors have occurred in the reproduction of some of the artwork in this text, which we were unable to correct before going to press. Please use copies shown here when referring to Figures 1.1 (page 6), 1.3 (page 10) and 3.6 (page 47). The publisher apologises for the inconvenience.

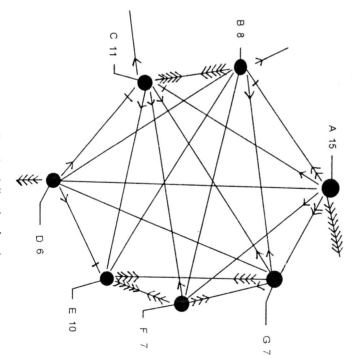

Figure 3.6 *Completed directional sociogram*

Options 2 and 3 will depend on the observing policy you and the group are to adopt. This is covered in Chapters 3 and 5 on observing activities.

Whichever option you choose, and this is particularly the case when you are in the same room as the learning group(s), unless you have a specific contract with the learners to do so, you should intervene, comment (either verbally or non-verbally) or interrupt as a last resort only. Your intervention might be premature or it may be resented by the learners who have taken ownership of the activity. Unless the activity is going badly wrong you should restrain any intervention you want to make and leave the group or pair to get themselves out of the wrong path or other difficulty. Self-correction will help them to learn much more than a teaching intervention by you. Even if things are going drastically wrong or the activity is falling apart, there are more appropriate interventions you can make than simply speaking up and interrupting the activity. Such methods are described well by John Heron (1995) in terms of prescriptive, informative, confronting, cathartic, catalytic and supportive interventions, although considerable care must be taken with many of these forms of intervention, whether authoritative or facilitative.

References

Elgood, C (1993) *Handbook of Management Games*, fifth edn, Gower.

Heron, J (1975) *Six-category Intervention Analysis*, University of Surrey.

Rae, L (1993) Activities for Trainers – bane or boon. *Training Officer*, Vol 29, No 10, December.

3
—

Group Activity Observation

One of the principal reasons for the all too frequent reduction in the value of practical activities in learning is the under- or misuse of, or even failure to use at all, any form of review following the activity. Early use of activities treated the activity as all, with learning considered an almost magical part of the activity. But in many cases as much, if not more learning emerges from a review or discussion of the activity as from the activity itself. Those reviews which are conducted are barren without a realistic observation of the process of the activity on which an in-depth analysis might be based. It is clear, then, that observing what happens in an activity is an essential part of the learning process.

STRATEGIES FOR OBSERVATION

A number of alternative strategies for observing the activity exist, the precise form often depending on the activity itself, the availability and skill of observers, the time available and so on. The alternatives include:

- no external observation;
- observation by the trainer;
- the use of observers;
- fishbowl observation;
- remote observation and CCTV;
- the use of video recordings.

No external observation

On some occasions, because the activity requires the involvement of all the learners or some other resource-restrictive reason, it may not be possible or perhaps desirable to have any observation at all of an activity. There must nevertheless be a review following the activity, but in this case reliance must be placed on the awareness of the participants themselves to enable a review to take place. Usually this takes the form of bringing together the participants – for example when a number of activities have been taking place simultaneously in different locations – to hold a discussion of what they noted, either directly or indirectly, and to help a summary of the learning from the activity to emerge.

Reliance on this approach has many dangers, particularly those of omission of learning points, misinterpretation of process events and sometimes failure to see what happened, even though that part of the process might have been highly significant. These omissions are quite natural, particularly if the activity is an interesting one in which the learners immerse themselves completely. Consequently the act of process, rather than the process itself, becomes all-important and all-exclusive in their minds. There are methods that can be used to support this approach and these will be discussed in Chapter 6 dealing with reviews.

Observation by the trainer

An immediate assumption will be that this must be the most effective observation because the trainer will be fully skilled at all aspects of observation. If the trainer is skilled in this way the observation should be realistic, unbiased and comprehensive, although the accuracy of the observation will also depend on the acuity of the trainer.

Even if the trainer is a skilled and experienced observer, this does not guarantee success as there are many pitfalls. Trainers are people and consequently have internalized value judgements, likes, dislikes and biases, and consciously or unconsciously may allow these to influence their observations. If they are obvious during the subsequent reviews the observations may be rejected by the learners, however accurate they may in fact be.

Some of the other dangers for the trainer-observer can be:

■ *The 'if you were me' syndrome* – if the learning group is not performing as well as they could or should do, you can too easily identify with the action and say (or at least feel during the observation) that you would have done it differently (better!).
■ *Over- or under-criticism* – depending on your attitude the learners can make accusations of over- or under-criticism because either you have been looking too critically at their performance during the activity, or you have not been watching with sufficient awareness.

They might feel that you are trying to protect them by taking a 'soft' attitude to them (paternalism) or trying to make them feel small by being unfairly over-critical.

■ *Multi-group observation* – in many training situations where activities are introduced you will be working with more than one group involved in activities simultaneously in several locations. You can only be in one place at one time. Your choices, if you are the lone trainer, will be to:

   a) observe none of the groups;
   b) observe one group only for the period;
   c) move between the groups for short periods with each.

The problems of (a) have been discussed. If you stay with one group only the other group(s) may react against this apparent favouritism and the observed group may feel that they are being singled out unfairly and will receive too in-depth a criticism compared with their peer groups. An approach as in (c) would appear to give you the best chance of seeing what each group is doing, but you may miss significant incidents when you are not with a particular group and, in the review, if you criticize the group for not doing something they might respond with the comment that they did this when you were not there.

Of course, the simple answer would be to have more than one trainer acting in an observational role, each with a group. This may be possible, in which case many of the criticisms are overcome, but in the case of the division of the learner group into several activity groups, a number of trainers may not be available.

■ *Non-intervention* – one of the principal dangers you will be open to when you act as an observer (or when you are sitting back letting learner-observers carry out the observation) is that you might be tempted to intervene in the activity. This temptation usually arises when you can see that they are taking the 'wrong' path. If this erring from the path continues, you will be tempted even more to intervene and help them back to the correct process. But you must remember that the purpose of the activity is to help them to learn: we learn as much (if not more) from our mistakes as from the things we do correctly. So, eventually, the erring group will find that they have taken the wrong path and a major learning will be how they retrieve the situation.

Of course, there will be occasions when it becomes obvious that if the group is allowed to flounder on it will soon fail, with a definite lowering of confidence and an absence of learning. If you are completely convinced that this is going to happen you must intervene or the time utilized will be completely wasted. However, there are appropriate ways to intervene:

- do not tell them that they are going wrong;
- do not tell them what they should do;

rather

- suggest that they should consider whether they are following an effective path;
- suggest that they may consider looking at such-and-such an approach;

then withdraw and allow them to reconsider their approach.

You must remember above anything that intervention by you must be the last resort, as such an interruption will be viewed by the learners as an attack on their abilities – even if they recognize that they are not succeeding! There will, however, be occasions when it is obvious that the activity is failing beyond any saving and you must decide to bring it to a halt. Even in drastic circumstances such as this, something can be saved. After the stopping of the activity and a short break to allow the members to return to the real world, a discussion can be started about what happened, why it happened and how it could have been done otherwise. After this discussion it may be acceptable to suggest that the activity might be repeated.

The use of observers

One alternative to the approaches described above is to use learners as observers, but in a more dedicated way than simply relying on them to observe as the activity proceeds. Observers in this case are selected from the learners and extracted from the activity group itself. The result of this is that eventually, you, have a band of observers who can relieve you of this task and be particularly helpful in a multiple activity situation. In most cases, unless the observers are particularly inept at giving feedback, the learners are more likely to accept comments and criticism from their peers than from you. One danger, similar to that when you are observing and reporting, may be that they will be too kind or too hard in their review – too kind because they do not want to hurt the feelings of their colleagues, or they know that at some time the others will be observing and reporting on them; too hard because they may feel that they shouldn't be too soft on their peers, or perhaps a previous experience might be colouring their attitudes.

Training the learner-observers

In order to ensure that the learner-observers are as effective as possible, you must take certain supportive actions with them. These will include the following.

Briefing. The observers must be thoroughly briefed before the activity commences, not only about what is required of them and how they might go about their observations, but also – in most cases – what the activity group is to do and any particular aspects of performance they should be looking for. It is very easy to take some of these aspects for granted.

Briefing can take a number of forms.

- The observers can be formed into a group and briefed by you in the required terms of: what the activity is all about, what their roles are, what they should be looking for, how they could record their observations, what will be expected of them in a review and feedback period.
- The observers, while the activity groups are reading their briefs, can, in an observer group, also read the activity briefs and any other observer briefs you might have prepared. You should also be available to answer any questions they might have.
- In addition to either of the above, the observers as a group might decide the methods of their observation, formulate their own observation forms, allocate responsibilities and so on. Again you should be available to support them in their deliberations.

Allocation of roles. Whether or not you have given the observers the responsibility for determining their own roles in the observation, you should ensure that certain functions are covered.

- The observers, being aware of the activity and the roles and functions of the participants, will also be aware of the objectives of the activity as far as the participants are concerned. Part of their brief must be to observe the movement towards and the achievement, or otherwise of these objectives.
- In many activities the participants will either be given or will take

on roles – the observers should decide who will observe certain role functions in the group being observed.
- Many activities have multiple objectives concerned with achievement of the task and also the people relationships that develop during the process – it may be decided that one observer looks at the task process and another at the people process.
- If a chairperson or leader is appointed for the activity, or during the activity this becomes part of the group process, the observers may allocate one of their number to observe the chairperson/leader, and another or others to observe the members. The tasks of the observers will be different in each case and help must be given to them in identifying these differences. Different checklists are useful in these instances to suggest the different roles being performed and consequently the varying behaviours to observe.

Non-intervention. Similar advice to that given earlier to trainers must be given to the learner-observers as they may be even more tempted to intervene or take part in the activity, particularly if they find they like the activity. Their role as an observer, who might miss significant events if they are involved, should be stressed.

Training for observation

One of the arguments levelled against the use of the learners as observers, usually by their fellow-learners, is that their observational feedback is wrong, principally because they, unlike the trainer, are not trained observers.

The solution, if it is possible within the time scale of the training event, and worth it because there are a number of occasions when observers will be used, is to include in the training programme training in observation. The learners can be guided by you in the ways of observation, the advantages and dangers (as described here), then some time devoted to practice before they are asked to perform 'real' observation. One very useful method I have found for this, which is not too demanding in these early stages of their learning observational skills, is the fishbowl technique described in the following section. Feedback techniques can also be included in time devoted to this topic and again the practice observations can be used to preface practice feedback sessions. Again the trainer should take a low-profile intervention in these activities, the learners being allowed (with support) to perform the observations and, importantly, to receive feedback on their observations and subsequent feedback from the learners on whom they have practised.

If there is no time available to give the learners some degree of training in observational skills you must question whether you should in fact allow the use of unskilled learner-observers, who may do more damage than anything else.

The fishbowl

The fishbowl approach is both a method of practising activities and one which helps in the learning of observational techniques and skill, as suggested above. The approach is effectively as the name suggests. A group of learners sit, usually in a circle, to perform some form of activity – a discussion on a subject, on which it is known that the individuals will have conflicting views. The group discusses the subject, (or otherwise performs the activity) for a set period of time – usefully 10 to 15 minutes, particularly if it is being used as a learning event for observation. The participants can be given roles or left to be themselves; a chairperson or leader may or may not be appointed or encouragement given for such a role; a subject can be given to the group or they may wish to select one themselves if they feel it will satisfy the activity criterion; and so on.

Seated outside the participant-group circle is a similarly sized group of observers. Each observer selects or is allocated an individual in the participating group. This is the person they observe under the guidelines for which the activity is being held. One observer looks at the

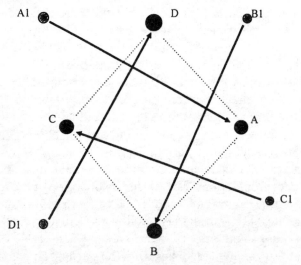

Figure 3.1 *Fishbowl observation*

chairperson/leader, the others at all the others of the group. It may be that there will be insufficient observers for this one-to-one observation – in such cases one observer might look at two members, but no more than this unless the observers are experienced.

As in any other form of observation the observers must be very clear about their roles and the areas in which they are to observe – task process or people process. Guideline instruments might be used, or the areas of observation left to the observers – again this may be normally only with experienced observers.

Following the end of the activity the observers, perhaps after a short observer-group discussion to decide on feedback strategy, give feedback to the people they have observed.

The roles are then reversed, with the original participant group becoming the observing group, and the process is repeated so that the full learning group has had the opportunity to practise observation and feedback. A useful activity for the second occasion, if it is relevant to the situation created by the first 'fishbowl', is for the second group to discuss or take action on one aspect raised by the first group, but the variations are extensive.

Remote observation

One of the problems encountered in observation is the effect of external observers on the activity participants by, obviously noting their actions. Some people feel that this can be offputting to the participants, particularly if the activity is or becomes personal in nature. This can have the effect on some people of making them behave in a way that is not their natural behaviour, perhaps withdrawing rather than saying something in front of somebody whom they know is listening intently to them, or perhaps behaving atypically by exhibiting unusual, extrovert behaviour.

Two principal approaches can be used to attempt to avoid these diversions: one-way glass and closed-circuit television (CCTV).

One-way observation

Although not used as frequently as in the past, this is a very useful technique which avoids the embarrassment of a third party being present during an activity. There are problems in its use because it requires custom-made glass and two rooms capable of having lighting variations introduced. It has its parallels at such security controlled places as airports where, for example, immigration authorities can observe incoming passengers through a glass window without themselves being seen.

In the training situation, the participants in the activity are in a well-lit room with no observers present. The observers, for example the remainder of the learning group, are in a nextdoor room separated by glass which permits one-way viewing only. As a result, the observers can see the participants, but not the other way round. Of course, the participants know they are being observed and there may be some awkwardness and artificiality in the early stages, but soon, particularly if the activity is absorbing, they forget about the observers and behave naturally.

The observers, supported by the trainer, will observe the participants in whatever way has been decided, including a modified fishbowl approach.

CCTV

The use of closed-circuit television can in many ways be considered the updated version of the one-way glass as it enables remote observation with the advantages of this as described above. Instead of the observing group watching the participants through the one-way glass, a video camera in the activity room projects a picture on a monitor or monitors for the observers who may be in a room or rooms in any other part of the building. Otherwise, the CCTV is the same as the one-way glass.

One major problem for many people is the obtrusive presence of a video camera and their knowledge that this is projecting a picture of them that can be seen by other people. Although there are some people who maintain this feeling, however long they are participating, most people soon forget all about the camera's presence, or stop acting unnaturally for effect, and behave naturally.

Apart from the actual presence of the camera in the activity room there is a further possibly unsettling effect. It is often necessary to move the camera by remote control so that it shows different views, or to change the zoom amount of the camera lens. Some cameras do this with a mechanical operation noise which can be very disconcerting. One method of avoiding these movements and their accompanying noise is to have more than one camera mounted, with appropriate lenses fitted so that every aspect can be seen with clarity. The cameras in use can be switched by an operator (frequently the trainer) located in the room where the observers are situated.

Video recording

The use of a video camera and recording equipment is a variation of the CCTV approach described above and in fact CCTV can be extended by the addition of a video recorder in the observation as well as using the facility for direct observation. The video recording can be used in conjunction with the observer comments in the feedback session. Again the participants may suffer temporarily because they know their actions are being recorded, but this nervousness usually only remains for a short period.

At one time CCTV was the only means of observing/recording because the equipment was so bulky, taking up so much room and being so obtrusive if it had to be in the same room as the participants. Modern equipment of high quality is much smaller and consequently more flexible and less obtrusive. The camera(s), either directly or remotely controlled, can be placed on tripods in the activity room with the control and switching equipment (and its operator) well away from the group. Long-focus lenses can also be used to move the camera away as far as possible, although this might create other technical problems.

OBSERVATIONAL METHODS

The observation of an activity participating group, whether carried out by you or by the learner-observers, can be done in a number of ways. Some more effective than others, often depending on the skill and experience of the observer – the greater the skill and experience, the less reliance on aids will be necessary and/or the more complex can be the observation.

Unguided observation

In such cases the observer, usually an experienced trainer, simply observes the activity group – whether directly or via remote techniques – no checklists or other guides are used other than the knowledge of the observer gleaned from their experience. You have usually constructed or selected the activity yourself and consequently know well the objectives and the learning points involved. As a result, if you are convinced that this is so, you will have no need for any memory joggers or *aide-mémoires* to help you with the observation. As the activity progresses you will be able to note critical and significant incidents and behaviours in a manner that you have developed over a period of time.

This may include comments as the activity proceeds, notes made under headings and activity blocks that you have retained mentally or even, if you are practised in this, the use of mind-patterns or spidergrams.

If you are completely convinced of your ability to cover everything in this unguided way then you will feel comfortable continuing in this manner, but most trainers, even very experienced ones, prefer to have some form of checklist or other observational guide to act as a supplement or safety factor.

Using observational guides

As suggested above, either you or your learner-observers can usefully use some form of guide or checklist to help them during their observations. Three major approaches are available as alternatives:

- observer-constructed checklists;
- pre-prepared checklists;
- activity analysis instruments.

Observer-constructed checklists

This approach is where the elected/selected observers are brought together – each observer from each group taking part in the activity – and given the opportunity to develop their own instruments of observation. This has major advantages:

- the observers have a sense of owning the checklist;
- the checklist can be customized to the activity;
- the observers will be more aware of the checklist content than if one is presented to them.

Obviously the observer group must be given the maximum amount of information possible about the activity in order to construct an observation aid. You should furnish them with the objectives of the activity and copies of the briefs given to the participants. From this information the observers – with your help as necessary – should be able to identify the major learning points and give indications of the possible approaches the participants might follow. As suggested earlier, different checklists will need to be constructed for the chairperson/leader and the other members.

Pre-prepared checklists

The comments made for the occasions when the observer group is constructing its own checklists apply equally when guides or checklists previously prepared by the trainer or activity constructor are provided. The questions or statements must be clear, relate to the activity and *must be capable of being observed with a minimum of interpretation*. Behaviours and activities should be *identified* and recorded as such – interpretation should be left for the feedback discussion that will follow the activity.

The actual checklists will vary depending on the type of activity being observed; and whether the leader or the members are being observed the checklist should also contain brief instructions to remind the user of the requirements even though the activity will often have been preceded by a discussion of some nature with or between the observers.

Figure 3.2 is an example of a fairly universal checklist for an observer who has to observe the chairperson or leader of an activity. A guide to be used in the construction of checklists is to include sufficient material to enable realistic feedback to be given, but not to much that the observer feels the 'yuk' factor when they see the list. This guidance is vague – necessarily so as the complexity of the checklist will depend on the activity itself, the time of the activity at a point in a programme and the experience/skill of the observer. Better too little than too much, since if there are a lot of notes made an observer may feel bound to comment on everything, which may destroy the value of the feedback.

Figure 3.3 is a similar checklist which would be used in observing the membership of a group performing an activity. The instrument–construction comments made for a leader observation checklist apply equally in this case. If a number of observers are to observe a number of participants – as for example in a fishbowl – it is essential that the same checklist is used so that inter-participant comparison can be made. Of course, if the participants are given widely different roles with prescribed behaviours, this will have an effect on varied checklists.

Observation Checklist for the Chairperson/Leader's Actions in a General Activity

It is your responsibility as observer to record comments on critical and significant events during the activity, so that feedback can be given after the activity to the participants. Do not take part in any way in the activity, whether verbally, non-verbally or physically. Do not try to record everything, only those aspects that appear to you as the most important ones.

How was the activity explained to the group?

Was an opportunity for clarifying questions given?

Unless set, how were goals, aims and objectives determined?

How was the organization for the activity made?

To what extent were the members given the opportunity to express their ideas?

How much did the leader take account of these suggestions?

How were the final decisions made, and by whom?

Were the existing resources – people and things – used effectively?

Was information about previous relevant experience sought?

How was the activity led?

To what extent, and how, did the leader try to motivate the members?

How effective was the leader's communication with the group?

Was everybody utilized in the activity?

What were the good aspects of the leadership?

What were the less good aspects of the leadership?

Was the task achieved?

On a scale of 6 (good) to 1 (poor), how would you rate the leader?

Any other comments on events during the activity for which the leader was responsible.

Figure 3.2 *Chairperson/leader observation checklist*

Observation Checklist for the Members' Actions in a General Activity

It is your responsibility as observer to record comments on critical and significant events during the activity, so that feedback can be given after the activity to the participants. Do not take part in any way in the activity, whether verbally, non-verbally or physically. Do not try to record everything, only those aspects that appear to you as the most important ones.

Did the activity purpose appear to be understood by the group?

Were any clarifying questions asked?

To what extent did the members involve themselves in the organization for the activity?

To what extent did the members express their ideas?

How much did the leader take account of these suggestions?

To what extent did the members involve themselves in the final decisions?

Were the members' knowledge, skills and expertise used effectively?

Was information about previous relevant experience volunteered?

How did the members react to the leader's leadership?

How motivated were the members?

How effective was the group's communication with
   the leader
   the other members?

Did everybody take an active part in the activity?

What were the good aspects of the members' activities?

What were the less good aspects of the members' activities?

Was the task achieved?

On a scale of 6 (good) to 1 (poor), how would you rate the group in this activity?

Any other comments on events during the activity for which the members were responsible?

Figure 3.3 *Members' observation checklist*

If the fishbowl approach is used the observers can be given observation checklists similar to that in Figure 3.3 with the questions aimed specifically at the member to be observed by each individual – 'Did he/she...?', 'To what extent did he/she...?'

INTERACTIVE BEHAVIOUR OBSERVATION

Observation of group activity is not always concerned with the task process and, in fact, what is often more relevant is not what they do, but how they do it – the behavioural aspects of people's actions. This area, however, is a much more difficult one than direct task process observation and will more usually – although not completely – be undertaken by you as the more skilled and experienced observer. One of the reasons for the difficulties is that you will be observing the behaviour of people, behaviour which is not always what it seems and which is only too easy to interpret rather than simply identify. Interpretation can easily be wrong, but identified and reported behaviours can be discussed with the result that there is a better chance of their real meaning coming to light.

Learners can be taught in a relatively short time to act as behavioural observers at a fairly restricted level, but there is rarely time, except for example in trainer training programmes, to enable them to reach a high skill level. Behavioural observation should be one of the skills of the trainer because in so many cases you will be involved in the interactions and relationships of the learners on your programmes, sometimes to a much greater extent than with the task process.

SIMPLE CONTRIBUTION SCORING

The simplest form of observation and subsequent analysis of a group's behaviour is known as simple contribution scoring. As the name implies this is concerned with the frequency with which a member of a group makes a contribution – in other words, says something. A contribution, of course, need not be only verbal, but non-verbal observational analyses are usually separate events.

The names of the group members are written on a sheet of paper. As the event progresses and a member speaks, ie makes a contribution, a stroke is made against that member's name. The end result is that you have a set of strokes against each member's name indicating how many contributions each made during the event. 'Five-barred gates' can be used to summarize sets of five contributions to make scoring addition easier. Figure 3.4 demonstrates a simple example of this observational approach.

Fred	ⅼⱧⱧ ⱢⱧⱧ ⱢⱧⱧ ⱢⱧⱧ ⱢⱧⱧ ⱢⱧⱧ ⱢⱧⱧ ⱢⱧⱧ ⱢⱧⱧ ⅼⅼⅼⅼ	49
Jean	ⱢⱧⱧ ⅼⅼ	7
Harry	ⅼⅼⅼ	3
Sally	ⱢⱧⱧ ⱢⱧⱧ ⱢⱧⱧ ⱢⱧⱧ ⅼ	21
Mary	ⱢⱧⱧ ⱢⱧⱧ ⱢⱧⱧ ⱢⱧⱧ ⱢⱧⱧ ⱢⱧⱧ ⱢⱧⱧ ⱢⱧⱧ ⱢⱧⱧ	45
Rita	ⅼ	1

Figure 3.4 *Simple contribution scoring*

This observational record shows the level of contribution for each member of the group, high, medium or low. Often chairpersons at meetings or leaders of other events feel at the end of the event that some people have been quiet or talkative, but do not know exactly how quiet or talkative. The leader and the other members may not even know that someone has been so quiet, or even quiet.

However, the record does little more than quantify the contributions in bare numerical terms. What it should do is raise questions for discussion, eg if Rita was as quiet as is shown, why did she not come in more? Was it because other, very high contributors did so much talking that she had no chance to enter the discussion – and presumably was never asked to do so by the leader? Similarly, why were Fred and Mary allowed to get away with dominating the discussion – was one of them in fact the leader?

This type of record does not show the length of the contribution – Fred's may have been mainly one-worders – nor does it give any indication of the quality of the contributions or how the discussion flowed. To obtain this sort of information different types of observational records are required. For example, one variation can be to place a stroke for every 10 seconds of a contribution (10 seconds being a period of time that you can easily estimate); or the sequence of the contributions can be shown by entering 1, 2, 3 and so on, as each contribution is made. Obviously, the greater the number of members in the group, the more difficult the recording becomes, but skill can quickly be attained in this form of observation, and 100 per cent completeness is not always essential.

DIRECTIONAL SOCIOGRAMS

If the observation has different objectives, eg to record the way in which the group discussion moves between the members of the group, in addition to the quantitative analysis found in the simple scoring approach a directional sociogram might be an appropriate instrument.

In this case a sheet of paper is configured with circles representing the members of the group in the relative positions in which they are seated. Before the observation, lines are drawn to join all the circles and a short line coming out of each circle in a direction away from the centre of the diagram. This initial chart would look like Figure 3.5.

Whenever a member of the group makes a contribution an arrow is placed on the line connected to the member to whom the contribution is made. If it is made to the group as a whole, the arrow is placed on the line pointing out from the contributing member. Additional information marks can be made such as a stroke across the line if the member interrupts another member. The number of arrows can be counted and these totals will, like the simple scoring, show the frequency of contribution, in addition to showing who were the contributors and to whom they made their contributions – to other individuals or to the group as a whole. Figure 3.6 demonstrates a completed directional sociogram – the numbers after the members' letters indicate the number of contributions made.

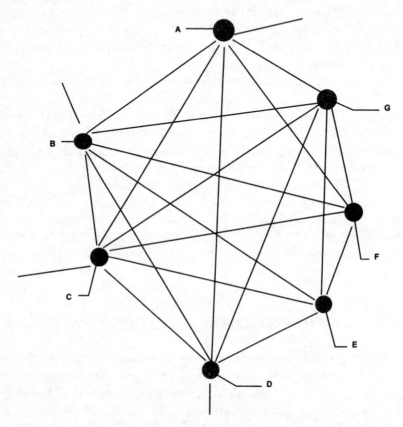

Figure 3.5 *Initial directional sociogram*

The sociogram shows that the particular activity observed in fact divided into four subgroups. Member D was almost completely isolated, being interrupted by members C and E, the only members to whom D was able to speak – but with little success! Finally D was reduced to making contributions to the group as a whole, but nobody replied. B and C formed a subgroup of two, in the main speaking only to each other. E, F and G formed a further subgroup, ignoring the remainder of the group most of the time. The leader, A, was ignored most of the time by D, E, F and G, interrupted by B and C and, like D, was forced to make most contributions to the group as a whole – again mainly being ignored.

These are some of the more straightforward and simpler forms of observation analysis which, although useful, give restricted information. In the next chapter a much more versatile and informative instrument is described, although still one which can be used by trainers and learners alike, the latter needing only a little instruction in some of its forms.

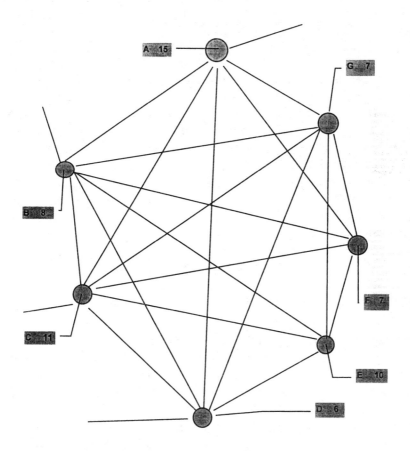

Figure 3.6 *Completed directional sociogram*

4

—

Behaviour or Activity Analysis

Both types of observational instrument discussed in Chapter 3 are very restricted in the amount of information they record for analysis and feedback. To be able to offer realistic feedback after the activity it is necessary to record events in both a quantitative and a qualitative way. Learners are not only interested in how often they had something to say, but also what they said, what effect it had and how valuable the contribution was. To give all this information would require a recording instrument that would be far too cumbersome to use, so some compromises have to be made. Behaviour analysis is such a compromise.

BEHAVIOUR ANALYSIS

Researchers such as Rackham, Morgan, Honey and others, working initially in the air transport industry, developed a practical approach to activity analysis (Rackham and Morgan, 1977; Rackham and Honey, 1971). This approach, which they called 'Behaviour Analysis', is relatively simple and straightforward, and extremely flexible in its use and application. The method is particularly useful in interpersonal or interactive skills development programmes, but can be used readily in any situation where the reactions and interactions of people are involved.

This interaction observation method involves recording the incidences of agreed sets of behaviour within a group and extends considerably the simple contribution scoring referred to in the previous chapter.

The behaviour is identified in categories, with each category capable of modification to suit the situation as long as certain criteria are observed:

■ meaningful to the observer and the observed;
■ readily identifiable behaviour;
■ high inter-observer reliability;

- categories that are distinct from each other;
- categories that have a relationship to the outcome.

I have used Behaviour Analysis (BA) extensively in my own training activities and have found it a superb instrument for observation and analysis. Some of the original categories I have added to or modified for my approaches or because they were not as clear for me as they could have been. These have been particularly concerned with: 'disagreeing', a category that I have separated into 'disagreeing without giving reasons' and 'disagreeing, giving reasons'. I see these as two separate behaviours, one negative, one positive. 'Defending/attacking' was reduced to 'attacking' as the single word seemed to me to describe both behaviours for the base reason. Similarly, 'blocking/difficulty stating' seems to cover a wide behavioural area of 'blocking' – simply impeding the progress of the activity or making statements that do not help the process. Although I use the word 'shutting-out' in most cases, in the majority of instances 'interrupting' seems to be the principal part of this behaviour.

The categories I use in general group activity observation, some of which are the original categories and some my own developments, are as follows.

- *Proposing*: A behaviour that puts forward, as a statement, a proposal or idea for a new course of action.
- *Suggesting*: Where the proposal is put forward in the form of a question – 'How do you feel if we do...?' Research by Honey showed that proposals put forward in this way have a higher incidence of acceptance than direct statement proposals.
- *Building*: A supportive proposal that extends or develops and enhances a proposal made by another person.
- *Seeking information*: Questioning behaviour aimed at seeking facts, opinions, views, ideas, feelings or information from others.
- *Giving information*: A stating behaviour that offers facts, opinions, views, feelings or information without developing into a positive proposal.
- *Disagreeing with reasons*: A statement of view that involves a conscious or direct declaration of difference of opinion with another's views, positively stating the reasons for the disagreement.
- *Disagreeing*: A bald, blunt statement of disagreement without any reasons being given.
- *Supporting*: A conscious, declared statement of support for another person or their views.

- *Testing understanding*: An attempt, by questioning or restating, to check whether a contribution made by another has been understood or that person has said what they meant to say.
- *Summarizing*: A statement in compact form that collates the discussion and decisions made to that stage of the event or a previous event.
- *Open*: A behaviour in which the speaker accepts or admits an error or omission, or apologizes for their actions.
- *Blocking*: A contribution that does nothing to progress the discussion with a negative form of statement that offers no alternative proposal for action.
- *Attacking*: A behaviour statement that contains overt value judgements on another and has emotive and aggressive overtones.
- *Bringing in*: A direct, verbal, positive attempt to involve another person, usually by means of a question and naming that person.
- *Shutting out/interrupting*: A behaviour that excludes or attempts to exclude another by interrupting them, contributing when another has been brought-in but hasn't yet spoken, or when two or more participants engage in side discussions.

The behaviour analysis is performed practically by the observer sitting quietly away from the group, taking note of everything that is said and recording this on a BA sheet. The BA sheet requires a stroke or other mark to be made every time an individual makes a contribution and the observer identifies not interprets the content of the contribution. The actual format of the BA sheet and the categories observed will depend on the skill and experience of the observer as a BA observer, the number of activity participants, the reasons for performing the BA and any other activities in which the observer has to take part. Observers who are drawn from the learning group, unless an extensive BA training programme has been undertaken, should be required to complete a limited BA. Obviously the more limited the BA the more limited will be the information recorded and available for use in feedback. With training and experience the number of categories can be increased.

If the number of categories has to be decreased, the ones included should be those identified as being the more significant ones in the particular activity. For example, if a problem-solving and decision-making activity is being observed, a shortened list of categories might usefully include:

- Proposing
- Seeking ideas
- Seeking information

- Giving information
- Summarizing
- Interrupting
- Other behaviours.

The format of the BA observation sheet could be as shown in Figure 4.1. The vertical columns are allocated to the individual members with their names at the head of the columns. The horizontal rows are for the included categories. At each contribution a stroke is made at the junction of the relevant name vertical column and the category row. The number of categories included on this observation sheet, once the observers are aware of the meaning of the categories, should be capable of being observed and recorded with a minimum of instruction. An increase in the number of participants does not necessarily make the task more difficult: after all, in most discussions, for most of the time, only one person is speaking at a time. Of course, there will be occasions when several people are contributing at once, or the pace of discussion increases considerably, but these are lesser parts of a discussion period and require the observer to be more aware and speedier at recording.

Figure 4.1 can be used to demonstrate a number of aspects of the group under observation.

- The level of contribution in quantity is quite well balanced with the exception of Sally, who is much quieter than most of the members and comes out with no original ideas, being principally content to state her own opinions only.
- Jean is also quieter than most of the group, but unlike Sally she at least makes a proposal and is interested enough in the other members to ask whether they have any ideas – not a too common behaviour. She is also quite a pushing member, interrupting on almost 30 per cent of her contributions.
- Mike appears to be the most creative of the members, making a large number of proposals, although he interrupts frequently to do so.
- Ralph has a very similar pattern to Mike, although with a lower ratio of interrupting.
- Mary is the highest contributor and, although making some proposals, tends to rely on making statements only, interrupting frequently to do so. She, however, supports the leader with a summary.
- John is apparently the leader, or exhibits more leader behaviours, asking a lot of questions, not proposing to such a great extent, summarizing, and interrupting at a minimal level only.

Of course, these assessments from the BA record alone do not tell the complete story, and an experienced observer will supplement the more numerical information with anecdotal observations. But no other approach offers as much information on one sheet, provided some care is taken in the analysis.

	John	Mike	Sally	Jean	Ralph	Mary	Totals
Behaviour Analysis Activity .... Period of observation							
Proposing	9	15		1	15	4	44
Seeking ideas	5			1	1		7
Seeking information	16	6	1	5	15	19	62
Giving information	12	22	12	14	14	25	99
Summarizing	7					1	8
Interrupting	6	15	1	10	8	14	54
Other behaviours	11	15		6	10	10	52
Totals	66	73	14	37	63	73	326

Figure 4.1 *A limited BA sheet*

The more experienced BA observer will be able to record behaviours with more group members and also with more categories. The more categories, the more likely that the final information will, being more detailed, be rather more effective. But a point arrives when an increase in the format of the BA sheet is self-defeating – there are too many categories for the observer to keep up with and a number of contributions will be lost. A famous law will ensure that of the contributions lost, someone in the group will say later 'Oh, but I did make one of those category contributions' and another member will support this. The credibility of the BA record will then be reduced. I have found that for a general group observation of about eight to ten members I can cope satisfactorily with about 11 categories. Figure 4.2 – using the same total figures as in Figure 4.1 – shows the type of BA sheet I use under these circumstances.

The BA sheet will also be modified by the type of activity being observed, in the same way that the learner-observer sheets described earlier were modified with different questions. For example, in sales and negotiation training programmes, the categories could be related to the aspects of the subjects themselves:

- Stating features
- Stating benefits
- Seeking requirements
- Resolving difficulties raised
- Closing
- and so on.

Behaviour Analysis Activity .... Period of observation							
	John	Mike	Sally	Jean	Ralph	Mary	Totals
Proposing	6	15		1	12	4	38
Building	3			0	3		6
Seeking ideas	5			1	1		7
Seeking information	16	6	1	5	15	19	62
Giving information	12	22	12	14	14	25	99
Summarizing	7					1	8
Open		1		1		2	4
Disagreeing		6		2	2	1	11
Attacking, blocking	1	8		2	6	6	23
Bringing in	10			1	2	1	14
Interrupting	6	15	1	10	8	14	54
Totals	66	73	14	37	63	73	326

Figure 4.2 *An 11-category BA sheet*

It may have been identified during a training needs analysis or it may emerge during a training programme that some aspect of a subject is causing particular trouble to the learners. Behaviour Analysis can help in this respect by concentrating on the suspected problem areas and producing analyses of these situations. For example, there may be problems in meetings at work or on a meetings training programme. The categories that would be helpful in such a case would produce a BA sheet as shown in Figure 4.3 in order to examine the proposing behaviour of the meeting group.

Behaviour Analysis Activity – Proposing Behaviour Period of observation	
Procedural proposals	
Content proposals	
Suggestions	
Building proposals	
Directive proposals	
Caught proposals	
Lost proposals	
Rejected proposals	
Repeat proposals	
Totals	

Figure 4.3 *Selective category BA*

A BA used in this way should be able to identify, or perhaps point the way to the problems arising in the meeting group. Or if it is suspected that the problems lie in other behaviours, similarly subdivided categories can be used.

BEHAVIOUR ANALYSIS IN ONE-TO-ONE ACTIVITIES

You will find that when you use Behaviour Analysis in one-to-one activities, such as interviews, the BA practice is easier than with a group as you have only two people to observe and record. This also means that the BA sheet you use can include more categories if required. The general categories described in Figure 4.2 can form the basis of such a BA sheet supplemented by other categories that relate more to the activity under observation, eg the one-to-one negotiation, the counselling interview, the discipline interview and so on.

In these cases only two recording columns are required; one for the interviewer and one for the person being interviewed. Part of such a BA is shown in Figure 4.4.

Behaviour Analysis **Activity – Problem-Solving Interview** **Period of observation ....**		
	INTERVIEWER	INTERVIEWEE
Procedural proposals		
Content proposals		
Suggestions		
etc		

Figure 4.4 *Part of a one-to-one BA sheet*

OBSERVATION OF THE INDIVIDUAL

It is sometimes desirable or necessary to observe the actions and behaviour of an individual in a group or other activity. All the methods described above and in the previous chapter can be used for this but, like the difference between group BA and one-to-one BA, the number of categories need not be as restricted as you will be concentrating on one person only.

Key notes

When recording incidents observed with an indivividual much more detailed notes can be taken, but you must be careful not to make these so full that you later find it difficult to extract the significant information for feedback. The most appropriate approach is to record key words and phrases that will remind you of the significant incidents.

The technique does require some practice. Initially many people, although identifying the key concepts, find it difficult to express these in key words and phrases quickly. As a result they write down too many words and consequently the listening can suffer.

It can be helpful if you do a lot of this type of activity observation and notetaking to construct your own set abbreviations, rather than learn shorthand or speedwriting. Some simple abbreviations could include:

+ or & – and	c – see or sea
ε – the speed version of 'e' or 'E'	q – queue
y – why	/ – the
1 – one	2 – too or two
4 – for	u – you
ur – your	b – be
r – are	-g – 'ing' ending
-n – 'ion' ending.	

There are also a number of standard abbreviations or literary conventions in common use that you can include in your own personal taxonomy:

eg – for example	ie – that is
cf – compare(d) with	→ – leads to, progresses to
> – is greater than	< – is less/smaller than
= – equals, is the same as	≠ – is not the same as, does not equal

These two chapters have described some of the principal methods of observation for use mainly with groups. There are of course others and the criterion to be established is whether or not the approach is valid, producing clear, unequivocal and as comprehensive as possible information about what has happened during the activity. Haphazard observing is worse than no observation at all, leaving any reporting open to accusations by the learners of bias, omission or error. Other variations will be considered later with the specific activities to which they refer.

References

Rackham, N and Morgan, T (1977) *Behaviour Analysis in Training,* McGraw-Hill.

Rackham, N and Honey, P (1971) *Developing Interactive Skills*, Wellens.

5
—

One-to-One Activity Observation

Many of the techniques described for use with groups can obviously be applied when you need to observe pairs functioning in an activity, such as practice interviews. In most cases it is simply a matter of scale – in the group you may be observing as many as 10 or 12 participants – and it will be readily seen that to concentrate on one or two people only makes the task much easier. In the same way that groups are observed, the observation can be performed by the trainer, the learners, remote observation and CCTV, and video recording.

LISTENING

One problem that exists when you are observing groups is continued with pairs, but the problem may be increased because of the small numbers involved and the more noticeable presence of the observers. This is your abillity to listen effectively and, although listening is a universal requirement in activity observation, it can often be a greater problem when observing pairs than in the case of groups. Often this is because when we are trying to observe, record and analyze the activities of a group we are kept on our toes because so much is happening. This activity heightens the need for our visual and aural senses to be as sharp as possible, and unless there are serious distractions we concentrate on the observation. When observing two people having a discussion or taking part in an interview, the environment is much quieter, the activity is frequently at a slower pace and the atmosphere is not as frenetic as can often be the case in a group activity.

Consequently more attention must be paid to the quality of the listening skills of the observer. Most people if asked will say that they are always listening, yet there is much evidence, direct or indirect, that this is not so. Listening, as with other human attributes, has barriers and problems that have to be overcome before that statement can be made realistically.

What is happening in so many cases is that when we appear to be listening we are really only hearing the voices and the words are in effect just washing over us. To listen effectively it is necessary to concentrate completely on the person who is speaking, to the exclusion of anything else. Unfortunately in practice we listen completely for a while, make assumptions about what is being said, and rather than continue to listen we start to interpret what we have heard, consequently not listening fully to what is then being said. We are fortunate that these multiple actions can be carried out to some extent, but if they are permitted to continue the diversions take over from the principal listening aim.

BARRIERS TO EFFECTIVE LISTENING

There are many barriers to effective listening, which are described widely in existing literature, so you or other observers must be aware of these to ensure that their effects are minimized.

The majority of listening barriers are overcome by the simple (!) expedient of making sure that we are concentrating 100 per cent on the interaction and not allowing extraneous factors to insert themselves between our brain and our ears. This is why as difficult an observing instrument that can be coped with is recommended, rather than a too simple one. Anything that can force us to listen to the process will help the total observation. Look for items on an extensive checklist, rather than take a simple approach; use the difficult patterned notetaking technique (easier for pairs than for a group); use a sophisticated BA sheet with a high number of categories of behaviour to observe; and so on. Chapter 4 contained some suggestions on the type of content for BA observation sheets for interviews.

An example of a specific-subject, general-format observation sheet for a one-to-one activity, in this case a paired negotiation, is given in figure 5.1. The observation sheet can be given to a nominated observer or observers prior to the activity, while the active participants are studying their role briefs.

Behaviour Analysis sheets of the nature described in Chapter 4 are ideal for one-to-one activity observations and, as commented on, much more detailed BAs, with more defining categories, can be used as only two people are being recorded. The negotiation activity observation sheet shown in Figure 5.1 can be extended into a BA sheet. This could take the form shown in Figure 5.2, with the general activities extended to include behaviour categories specific to negotiation.

Negotiation Observation Sheet

1. (Enter here, prior to handing over the sheet, the specific negotiation techniques that have been covered in the learning event and which you want the observers to watch as they are being carried out.)

2. How satisfied were you with the outcome of the negotiations?

    Extremely   Extremely
    satisfied   dissatisfied

6	5	4	3	2	1

    Why have you given that scoring? Give information on the outcome and the way it was approached.

3. How satisfied were you with the performance of the negotiators?

    Extremely   Extremely
    satisfied   dissatisfied

6	5	4	3	2	1

    Why have you given that scoring? Give examples of the negotiators' behaviours during the event.

4. Mark an 'x' above the number best describing one negotiator, for each dimension, and an 'o' above the number best describing the other.

    Flexible   Rigid

6	5	4	3	2	1

    Trusting   Suspicious

6	5	4	3	2	1

    Considerate   Inconsiderate

6	5	4	3	2	1

    Co-operative   Competitive

6	5	4	3	2	1

5. How willing would you be to negotiate with either party at some time in the future?

    Very willing   Very unwilling

6	5	4	3	2	1

    Why do you give this score? Please give any specific event comments that you can.

6. Any other observations you made during the negotiation.

Figure 5.1 *A negotiation observation sheet*

Behaviour Analysis Activity – Negotiation X Period of observation		
	Negotiator 1	**Negotiator 2**
Proposing		
Proposing alternatives		
Making hypothetical offers		
Suggesting		
Building		
Seeking ideas		
Seeking information		
Giving information		
Supporting		
Disagreeing		
Disagreeing with reasons		
Refusing		
Refusing with reasons		
Open		
Testing understanding		
Summarizing		
Blocking		
Belittling		
Threatening		
Interrupting		
Suggesting adjournment		
Totals		

Figure 5.2 *Negotiation activity BA sheet*

NON-VERBAL COMMUNICATION

Non-verbal communication (NVC), the way we communicate without words but with gestures, facial expressions and so on, is occurring all the time in any form of interaction between people, whether these are people in groups or in pairs. However, if you are observing a group for verbal behaviour, although you may notice some of the non-verbal signals, you will probably miss many more. Of course, you may specifically observe NVC rather than verbal behaviour, but then you may not catch all the verbal contributions.

The observation of NVC at the same time as verbal communication is made easier in a paired event, simply because you have fewer people to listen to and watch, so NVC becomes a more important and significant aspect of paired events.

The more important aspects of NVC as far as one-to-one activity observation are concerned are:

- gestures
- facial expressions
- gaze
- posture
- proximity.

Some aspects of these are described here.

Gestures

The variety of human gestures is very wide and expressive, although, as with any other NVC signal, we have to be careful in its interpretation. A signal that has a particular meaning in one culture or country can have a completely different (and sometimes completely opposite) meaning in another. Many are unconscious gestures and signal the attitude of the sender.

- A typical gesture is extending the hands towards the other person as you are speaking, the position of the palms making the difference. The palms upwards or towards the other person suggests that the speaker is being open.
- The 'baton' gesture can illustrate progressive intentions. The baton can be a pointing finger which when used by the speaker towards the listener is intended to be an emphasis, telling the other person to listen. If the finger is then wagged up and down while pointing

even more emphasis is made, plus a warning to the listener that they had better take notice. When the finger is being jabbed towards the listener, this is a signal that the listener must take account of what is being said (or else!).

■ Another gesture that can be linked with congruence or otherwise is facial stroking. These gestures can be used as delaying or 'displacement' movements when we are not ready to come out with (usually) disagreement with the other, or otherwise wish to delay or hide our feelings. Such a gesture occurs when it is our turn to speak and the chin is cupped by the hand palm, the elbow on the knee and the fingers pointing up the face. A rather different hand placement, where the index finger is placed on the cheek and pointing up, with the rest of the hand at the chin (often with the head tilted slightly) suggests that the listener is evaluating information given because it is interesting.

Facial expressions

■ The expressions that cross your face are frequently give-aways to the thoughts that are crossing your mind but not being expressed. A smile usually indicates agreement or pleasure, although the smile can easily be a false one, hiding the true feelings. A frown can indicate disagreement, but could also suggest that the frowner is concentrating their thoughts on something you have just said.

■ The eyes are said to be the windows to your soul. They can also be the windows to your inner and unexpressed thoughts. People who smile with their mouth but not with their eyes are usually looked on with suspicion. If you want to hide your amusement, you do not mouth-smile, but your amusement is often disclosed by the 'smile in your eyes'.

Eye gaze

■ The signals given by the eyes as they are used to look (or not look) at people can be very strong NVC indicators, but are perhaps the ones which are most often misinterpreted. For example, the person who very infrequently looks at the other person to whom they are talking may be hiding their feelings, may be 'shifty' or dishonest, but may equally be very shy and simply not like looking at the eyes of others unless they have a very close relationship with them. On the other hand, looking eye to eye does not necessarily mean the reverse, and if the gaze is too constant and direct, the receiver can be made to feel uncomfortable – this may be the intention of the gazer.

■ Just as significant as the length of the gaze, eye to eye, can be the geographical area of the other's face at which you direct your gaze. The 'business' gaze is directed at a triangle on the other's forehead, between but above their eyes. This suggests that you are looking at them, but do not want to be too informal by looking them 'in the eyes'. A social atmosphere permits this gaze direction to drop and is directed to an upturned, triangular area formed across the eyes and down to the mouth. A more intimate gaze is to an extended area from across the eyes, down to the mouth and continuing further down to the chest. Awareness of the type of gaze can be useful in identifying the relationship between the people taking part in the activity.

Posture

The posture that people assume when they are reacting with each other can often give indications of their unspoken thoughts.

■ Sitting upright in the chair with an alert expression usually indicates interest and listening.
■ Turning away from the speaker, perhaps with only the lower body, perhaps even including the head, can indicate disinterest to various degrees.
■ Sitting or standing with arms folded suggests a protective or other barrier attempt – research has shown that when the listener crosses their arms, their receptiveness to what the other is saying reduces by 40 per cent. If, with crossed arms, the fists are also clenched, this suggests a hostile or aggressive attitude.
■ Hand clenching or clenching the arms of the seat suggests frustration being held back; a slight forward movement in addition suggests that the person wants to express their feelings, but is still holding back.

Proximity

There is not always the opportunity for the two people involved in the activity to change their seating, often because they have to sit in particular positions because of video camera angles. But if there are no restrictions positioning and proximity can give good relationship signals.

- Voluntary positioning 'across the desk' usually signified a conflict (at most) or a formal (at least) situation, where the desk is a barrier between the two people. However, many people are so used to this seating arrangement that they accept it naturally without reading anything into it. The opposite is sitting side by side, a very social arrangement which indicates friendliness, openness and informality. The 'in-between' position in an interview is where the interviewee is placed diagonally across the desk, near the corner, either on the long or short sides. It is interesting and significant to observe where the seats are moved to if this is an option.

- Proximity can also be demonstrated by what are known as the 'proxemic zones'. These are the different distances that usually indicate the personal space that people require, and the distances that are allowed or accepted suggest the relationship or the offer of relationship. *Personal* space is reserved for family, relations and close friends, when the people can sit or stand very close together, and are even touching. *Social* space is when the situation is rather more formal, or when this is the impression that is to be suggested, and the proxemic distance is 'arm's length', about three feet or so. *Business* space has at least six feet between the individuals and is the formal situation, often assisted by having a desk between the two people. *Public* space is the largest zone and can vary according to the situation or to whether the desired space is possible. This is likely to be the least used of the proxemic zones found in one-to-one activities.

The foregoing has commented on some of the more common of the very extensive NVC signals observable in one-to-one situations and which can frequently be interpreted, or at least identified when they occur. However, NVC is difficult to interpret because the signals do not necessarily mean what they appear to indicate, eg the 'smile-mask'. The safest procedure is to look for clusters of behaviour – if the various behaviours in the cluster are congruent, interpretation can be more reliable. The instance of the listener leaning forward, hands partially extended and mouth slightly open, with an 'interested' facial expression, is usually safely interpreted as someone who wants to break in and make a positive verbal contribution.

You may have to decide whether observation is to cover verbal behaviour, non-verbal behaviour or both. The decision will be based on a number of factors related to the situation, among which are:

- the availability of observer(s);
- the experience of the observers – you or learner-observers;

- the type of activity;
- the objectives of the activity – whether the verbal or non-verbal processes are the most important;
- the time available for feedback of the many processes that can be observed in an activity;
- how the observations will be fed back to the participants.

Fuller information is available in Argyle (1988) and Morris (1978).

OBSERVATIONS OPTIONS

The options open for observation of one-to-one activities are very similar to those for group observation, although there is one important approach that will be introduced here and described further when role play activities are being described in Chapter 9.

The trainer as the observer

Most of the guidelines given for observation by trainers themselves given in Chapter 3 apply in the case of one-to-one activities.

Certainly, as commented earlier, intervention must be only permitted as a last resort, and even when this appears to be the case intervention must be delayed, as too early an entrance might stop the participants from solving the impasse themselves. Intervening and stopping the activity must be the ultimate option, preceded by attempts through limited intervention to encourage the participants to follow another course that would enable the activity to resume and continue.

Remote techniques in observation

The learners themselves can be used as observers of one-to-one activities in the same ways as for group activities, but with the caveats mentioned above because of the greater sensitivity of this type of situation. In most cases, the one-way window and the CCTV observation methods will be even more effective in observation of pairs performing an activity than in the case of observing groups. Certainly the participants will be aware of the remote observation – a group of peers on the other side of what appears to them to be a mirror or, more frequently, awareness of the camera in the room pointed at them and transmitting sound and vision to the group located elsewhere. Their nervousness is usually greater than when a group is being observed as the scrutiny of an individual is closer, particularly where the person is feeling unsure and lacking confidence.

Camera-shyness can certainly affect performance, sometimes to the extent of destroying any natural activity, or even any activity at all. But these are minority events: most people are initially nervous – even professional television performers suffer from starter nerves. But, like the professional performers, once the activity is under way and the participants become immersed in the activity process and features, the majority forget completely about the camera.

A number of measures can help to alleviate problems raised in these ways. The camera can be hidden behind an apparently opaque dome fitted to the wall, although because the dome is a physical feature the participants are still aware that a camera is behind it. But psychologically the hiding of the camera helps to lessen concerns.

One of the major problems reported by people taking part in video camera observed events is the distraction, particularly when they are starting to become immersed in the process, of camera movement. Some operator/observers have the camera close-focused on one or other of the pair at any time, usually the one speaking, to pick up non-verbal behaviours in addition to the words. Then the camera is swung, albeit slightly, to contain the other person who is now speaking. This movement, however silent, is still an alien movement and can be a distraction. Ideally the camera should be mounted and fitted with a lens such that both participants can be observed clearly and no direction or focusing movement is necessary. But this is not always possible and, people being people, if the ideal is achieved, half-way through the event the participants decide to move their chairs and positions!

In situations of this nature you must weigh up the advantages and disadvantages of live observers against video observation – where both resources are available.

In general, one approach that you can use to minimize the effect of camera obviousness is always to have the camera on show so that the learners can become used to its presence. I have used this approach and frequently the learners have asked if the camera can be used on occasions when its use was not intended. If this happens – agree!

The learning group as observers

Individual learners from the learning group can of course be used as observers, taking the place of the trainer, and all the comments made in the chapter on group observation and on the trainer's role above apply. Particularly strong rules should be laid down for these observers to remain as far from the sight of the participants as possible, to make their notetaking as unobtrusive as possible and, above all, not to intervene in any shape or form. It is not unusual for a learner-observer to become so excited by the event, or frustrated by what they can see clearly should be happening, that they intervene and interrupt the activity.

There is an alternative approach using the learners as observers, but one that must be used with care and only if you know very well the capabilities of the learning group. This involves one pair of participants performing at the front of and in the sight of the remainder of the learning group, this remainder acting as a group of observers. In some cases this can be an even more traumatic event than performing the activity in front of a video camera and of course it restricts the number of people who can take part in actual activities. This may be the only possibility in some situations, however, although, in spite of the truism that the observer sees more than the participant, I believe that maximum learning occurs when you experience something yourself.

Whichever form of observation using the learners as observers is used, observation forms should always be used and the observers encouraged to use them fully – memory is a most unreliable data source when it comes to feedback time. Certainly in the early stages of a learning event there should always be a period of time set aside before an activity for:

- the trainer to hold a mini-teach-in and discussion with the observers;
- the observers, if there are a several, to meet as a group, to read the activity brief and discuss this, and to ensure that they are *au fait* with the observation sheet;
- as part of learning, the observers to meet and produce their own observation sheets based on the key points of the subject and how different observers may look at different parts of the activity or different participant roles.

These observer activities can be taking place while the participants are studying their activity briefs. One of the problems frequently encountered is that one group – observers or participants – complete their studies before the other group and either, involuntarily, put pressure on the unfinished group, or become frustrated at having to wait. You will have to keep a careful eye on situations such as this and have other tasks prepared for the group that has finished early.

Triad observation

The most common method of observation of one-to-one activities is for a number of activities to be taking place concurrently, each pair having its own observer. If you are using all the learning group in rote as observers, some will be more adept as observers than others, and if the participants feel that their observer is not very adept, any observations may be viewed with suspicion or even rejection. One method of solving this problem, if it cannot be avoided, is to follow the practice of using two observers on each occasion – a quartet situation rather than a triad! Even this is not without its dangers as the two observers, because of their different perceptions, may eventually report different observations.

Triad activity observation

In addition to a triad approach to observation, there is a particular form of running one-to-one activities known as 'Triads'. This still uses the basic situation of three people, two participants and one observer, but in this case the observer has a role particular to the activity type. This will be described in Chapter 11.

References

Argyle, M (1988) *Bodily Communication*, Routledge.
Morris, D (1978) *Manwatching: A Field Guide to Human Behaviour*, Grafton.

6

—

Reviewing Activities

All aspects of an activity are equally important and essential, but if I had to choose one as the most essential I would select the review and feedback stage, the one following the performance of the activity. Of course, without the activity there would be nothing to review! The frequent reduction or omission of effective reviews can be due to a trainer's fear of the process and of being seen as ineffective before the learners. In other cases it is the activity alone that is considered to be the important aspect.

But as is drawn out so clearly in the learning approaches of Kolb, and of Honey and Mumford, complete learning does not occur with activity alone. Time and personal resource must be given to reflecting and theorizing, thinking about what has happened, with and to whom and with what results. Consideration must then be given to why this happened, what alternative options might have been available and what would have happened if other options had been taken. Finally, as a summary of the reflections and wider considerations, lessons can be learned and plans made for more effective implementation.

Inexperienced trainers tend not to appreciate the time needed for the effective review of an activity, time that can easily well exceed the activity itself. This will be particularly the case if several sub groups have taken part in the activity; have all to report their actions/findings; have observations heard and discussed; the group findings assessed, interpreted and agreed; and the learning from the activity summarized in learning points and developed into action plans. There is little wonder that the process requires a substantial block of time.

OPTIONS

The form of the review and feedback will depend on the nature of the activity, how observers were used, how interactive the event was, and so on, but whatever its form, its aim will be to enable the main learning points to be drawn out and discussed, with decisions being made from these discussions.

The options for the review process include:

- trainer-centred review *of* the group's activity;
- Behaviour Analysis;
- trainer-centred review *with* the group;
- group self-review;
- use of video recorded observation.

Trainer-centred review *of* the group

This approach was at one time the almost universally used method. Not that it was necessarily the most effective, but it gave the trainer complete control of the process, an approach that was thought to be essential at that time. At the end of the activity, for which the trainer or trainers involved had been the observer(s), the 'experts' gave their opinions from their observation notes. This is an option that is still used at times today, sometimes for legitimate reasons, although the consensus view is one that doubts the justification for a singular, prescribed, possibly biased (and even possibly incorrect) approach. Much will depend on:

- how skilled the trainer is at observing;
- how skilled the trainer is in recording all significant events;
- how skilled the observer is in analyzing the data;
- how skilled the trainer is in feeding back the observations;
- how credible the views of the trainer are with the group.

Feedback of this nature tends to be one way, in which the trainer passes on the observations and analyses to the group then moves on to the next event or activity, assuming that the learners have understood and accepted the feedback. The pseudo approach to interactivity is when, following the statement of the trainer's feedback, the group is asked for their reaction to the comments. If the feedback was highly supportive, the approach is likely to be met with little or no comment; but if it is critical (and badly expressed) a very negative type of response can be produced, with counter-criticism or even conflict. Nowadays people who attend developmental events do so to learn, not to be taught or taught-at, and being told what they did wrong or poorly can arouse strong feelings.

However, there are some occasions when this approach might be justified to some extent. If time is very limited, and with the best will in the world the trainer cannot afford a prolonged discussion, the bare statement feedback may be all that is possible. If this is the case with any of your training, you may be best advised to reconsider the planning of the content and use of time in your event, rather than risk the negative reactions of this type of review.

Behaviour Analysis

One less threatening form of prescribed or stated feedback is the use of Behaviour Analysis, which can be seen as an almost ideal instrument for giving feedback. It is (or should be) non-judgemental in its recording of the behavioural data accrued during the activity, although its value can easily be ruined by inept use in the feedback. As an apparently unbiased record of the behaviour of individuals it can, however, be seen as challenging by some. If the data is expressed verbally, even in a well-hidden, critical manner, the response can be negative.

I have found that an effective feedback reaction is more likely if a set of understandable data is produced and copies are distributed to the learners. Provided they have an understanding and appreciation of BA, the categories used and why they were used, they will be able to interpret the data themselves, with only explanatory comments by the trainer. The only other comments necessary by the trainer are concerned with assistance to the learners' interpretations *if they come to seek help*. Behavioural feedback is often found in interpersonal, interactive learning groups which, by the time sufficient data is available for feedback, have reached an appropriate interactive level so that they:

- can accept feedback data of their appropriate or inappropriate behaviour;
- want to discuss and share the feedback with others;
- want to know how they compare with an interactive model and/or the behaviour patterns of their colleagues.

Category / Activity	A		B		C		D		E		F		Average	
Proposing	2	2%	6	11%			3	16%	1	3%			2	5%
Suggesting			1	2%									–	–
Building			1	2%									–	–
Seeking ideas			1	2%									–	–
Seeking information	14	14%	9	17%	3	10%	1	3%	4	21%	1	3%	5	11%
Testing understanding	2	2%	1	2%									1	2%
Giving information	43	43%	23	43%	19	63%	24	77%	7	37%	16	43%	22	50%
Disagreeing + reasons	11	11%									1	3%	2	5%
Summarizing														
Supporting	5	5%	3	6%	1	3%	1	3%	1	5%			2	5%
Open	1	1%												
Disagreeing	1	1%									1	3%		
Attacking											2	5%		
Blocking	9	9%	2	4%	7	23%	1	3%	3	16%	7	19%	4	9%
Bringing in	1	1%									2	5%	1	2%
Shutting out	12	12%	6	11%			4	13%	1	5%	6	16%	5	11%
Number of your individual contributions in each activity / Number of contributions in the group in each activity	$\frac{101}{396}$	(26%)	$\frac{53}{250}$	(21%)	$\frac{30}{390}$	(8%)	$\frac{34}{249}$	(13%)	$\frac{17}{145}$	(12%)	$\frac{36}{289}$	(12%)	$\frac{44}{287}$	(15%)
(Average for group)	(59)		(36)		(56)		(35)		(21)		(41)		(41)	

Figure 6.1 *Behaviour Analysis profile for each individual*

73

The next stage is not feedback, but the natural result of this the action that the individuals and the group intend to take as a result of the feedback and their plans for modifying behaviour, both individual and group.

Figure 6.1 shows an example of a BA group feedback summary such as the one mentioned above. Delay in giving this feedback until a number of activities have been observed gives a more realistic behaviour pattern or profile than after each activity, as the behaviour of people varies considerably from one event to another – the activity may not appeal to them, they may know nothing about the subject of the activity, the time of day may be having an effect, something may have been said to them that is having an effect on their behaviour at any one time and so on. However the form of the feedback, in addition to identifying a pattern, also gives the opportunity for a look at the individual events and the variations from one to the other.

In Figure 6.1 the horizontal rows represent the behavioural categories over which the individual has been observed. The vertical columns give a wealth of information, recording the number of contributions made by the individual (the figure in the left of the box), and (in the right of the box) that raw figure expressed as a percentage of their total contributions in that activity. At the foot of the columns for each activity the figures show (a) the total of their personal contributions compared with the total contributions of the group and (b) that equation compared with the group average in that activity.

The final column averages out their behaviours in the same way. Thus the individual can see to what extent they contributed during each activity and what they said (the category), how they compared with the rest of the group in that activity, and a profile of their behaviour compared with that of the group over the total of events observed and recorded.

A number of analyses can be produced from the data in Figure 6.1. The figures show that the individual contributed to the group discussions initially at a higher rate than the group average – eg in Activity A the person contributed 101 of the group's 396 total contributions (the group average being 59), a percentage rate of 26 per cent and in Activity B a contribution of 53 of the group's 250 total contributions (the group average equalling 36) a percentage rate of 21 per cent. By the time the programme had progressed to Activity F, our individual's rate had decreased to 12 per cent with 36 contributions out of the group's 289 (group average equalling 41). The overall impression is that the individual was starting to control him/herself much more in the group situation and not making the lion's share contributions.

However, the total number of contributions is only part of the story, and it is necessary to examine the specific behaviours to gain a much more effective appreciation of any change. This examination shows that although the total contributions had changed by decreasing, there was little difference in the particular behaviours, and in fact some demonstrated a less than desirable pattern. This pattern suggests that about half, and sometimes considerably more, of the contributions are simply statements by the individual of his own views, opinions and knowledge at the expense of building a relationship with others and finding out what they feel – a self centred approach within the group. This is suggested by the overall 50 per cent rate for giving information, 9 per cent blocking behaviour and 11 per cent interrupting or shutting others out to make some of these statements. This compares with the 11 per cent rate of seeking the views of others, 5 per cent supporting behaviour, only 2 per cent bringing-in others and virtually no building supportively on the proposals made by others. The 5 per cent rate proposals suggest that although the individual has a lot to say, little of this comes out in a creative, constructive form of proposals for action.

Obviously a chart of this nature cannot give all information necessary for a complete behavioural picture, but it does at least give a factual basis for the start of a discussion and analysis by the individuals

In the case shown the Action Planning result of the feedback and subsequent discussion with the others of the group included the behavioural objectives to:

- control the amount of contributions in a group discussion or activity and so give others a chance to speak;
- make more positive contributions in the form of proposals and suggestions, and constructive builds on the proposals made by others rather than stick out at any cost to get personal proposals through;
- be more supportive of colleagues by giving active support and seeking more of their views and opinions;
- reduce any non-constructive views;
- reduce the amount of shutting-out (interrupting) and allow others to express their views, particularly when they have been sought.

Trainer-centred review *with* the group

This is a much more common and useful approach, with the trainer again taking the lead, but with considerably more group participation than in the first method. The principal difference is that questions are asked of the learning group rather than statements being made to them by the trainer. It can, however, fail very easily, usually if when the questions are asked, responses are few or not particularly open. It is most frequently used when the whole learning group, as one group rather than multi-groups, has taken part in an activity, although it can be used with more difficulty when a number of groups have been used.

The approach can be made more effective by trying to ensure that responses are full and open: normally achieved as a result of the type of questions the trainer asks. It is very little use asking bluntly and blandly 'How did you think that went?' The questions must be designed to draw out views, feelings, information and attitudes, and consequently must be designed as well as possible.

Many of the questions will relate, in structured activities and simulations, to the task itself, particularly if it was a work-related exercise, and the design of the review will need to include formulation of questions based on an understanding of the task itself. But in many cases the task is merely a vehicle in which skills and behavioural learning can take place. Consequently there will need to be a designed set of process questions. The number and type of questions, and to whom they are to be directed, will frequently depend on the situation, but much of the end result will rest on the trainer's skills and ability in designing the appropriate questions *and* knowing how to ask them. All participants should be actively included in the review – leader/interviewer, group members/interviewee and observer(s). The questioning should not be simply seeking straight information, but follow-up questions should extend or clarify the responses and draw out feelings and attitudes.

Group variations

If the complete learner group has taken part in an activity as one group, at the end of the exercise you should have the group return to their appropriate seating arrangement so that the review can proceed. You can then start posing the questions that you have designed, principally with the intention of starting a discussion about the learning achieved from the activity. The larger the group, the more difficult it will be to control the discussion and to ensure that everybody has an opportunity to make a contribution, and the easier it will be for deliberate non-contributors, shy and quiet members and those who may be deliberately evading issues to hide in the group. The secret of success, if indeed there is one, must be in as extensive a participation as possible of the learners, rather than an emphasis on your role.

Where a number of sub-groups have been performing the same

activity, at the end of the active period all groups are brought back to the main room for a similar review activity. However, because of the number of groups, a different approach must be taken as questions addressed to what is now the full group will only result in a confused discussion. Three principal options are available:

- seek the full, relevant information, etc from each group in turn;
- seek the full, relevant information, etc from each group in turn, but ask for statements of differences only after the first group's report;
- seek the information from each group in turn (specifying differences from the first reporting group only) by questioning the leaders in each group or pair, then the group members or interviewees, then the observers.

All these approaches will take much more time than was necessary with the review of one full learning group, but opportunity must be given for everybody to make at least their most significant comments, otherwise response will be less on the next review. The first of the three approaches summarized above is the most time consuming and the least effective as there is likely to be a lot of repetition from group to group. The second will tend to reduce this repetition, but even with the request for comments on differences only between groups there will be some as people want to contribute.

The third method introduces a greater element of control, and in this case more effectiveness in the review, as on each occasion smaller groups of people are being asked for their views. The most problematical group will obviously be the group members, the largest group and the one with the more disparate comments to make.

In many ways the review of one-to-one activities will be more controlled as each 'group' (usually the interviewer, the interviewee and the observer) is smaller and will normally be more self-disciplined. But the process for both group and one-to-one activities is very much the same – views being sought on what happened, what were the results and what learning has been achieved.

Effective questioning

It has already been mentioned that an effective questioning approach is most likely to ensure success in the review and this can be approached by having a basic set of questions designed before the event. The matter of task questions has already been mentioned, but the more difficult and frequently the more important are the process questions that show the extent of the learning. A possible format for reviewing the results of a problem-solving group is shown in Figure 6.2. The *aide-mémoire* should not be used as a list to be followed slavishly, nor need all the questions be asked – many responses may give the further information without the need for further questions. Use the list as a guide to ensure that, within the time available, all the relevant information emerges.

Leader Debrief Aide-Mémoire

1. What did you see as the specific objectives of the activity?
2. How successful do you feel you were in achieving these objectives?
3. What were the main problems that you encountered as leader and how did these occur?
4. How did you overcome the problems?
5. What did *you* do that hindered the process?
6. What behaviours/actions by the group members
    – hindered you and the performance of the task
    – helped you in the performance of the task?
7. If you had been a member, how would you have behaved/what would you have done?
8. If you had to repeat the activity, what changes would you make in how the group went about the task?
9. What learning have you extracted from the activity that you can take back to your workplace either in your own role or from the viewpoint of your manager?

Figure 6.2 *A leader debrief aide-mémoire*

A similar *aide-mémoire* can be constructed to help you in your questioning of the group members; this is shown in Figure 6.3.

Group Member Debrief Aide-Mémoire

1. What did you see as the specific objectives of the activity?
2. To what extent was the leader responsible for describing the objectives?
3. How well did the leader explain or clarify the objectives?
4. How successful do you feel you were in achieving these objectives?
5. How did the group go about agreeing the methods of operation?
6. How involved were all the members in reaching this decision?
7. How much were you personally involved?
8. Were any problems caused by the behaviour/actions of
    – the leader
    – other group members?

---

9. How did these arise?
10. How were they dealt with?
11. How effective did you feel you (the group) were (was) in the activity?
12. How effective did you feel the leader was?
13. If you had been the group leader would you have approached this activity in any other way?
14. To what extent were you involved in the activity?
15. To what extent did you feel part of the group?
16. If the activity was repeated, would you behave in any different way?
17. What learning have you extracted from the activity that you can take back to your workplace either in your own role or from the viewpoint of your manager?

Figure 6.3 *A group debrief aide-mémoire*

A number of the questions in Figure 6.3 relate to the group as a whole, the others to individual members seeking their personal views. Some of these questions might be omitted depending on the circumstances, the time available and the type of activity being reviewed. Normally you would construct an *aide-mémoire* for both these types of purposes, but they are combined here so that the *aide-mémoire* can be referred to later.

If observers have been used, they will have been observing the group activity and the leader from the observation brief in use. Questioning of this group of participants can follow the observer brief or a questionnaire devised from parts of this.

Reviewing one-to-one activities

The comments made above in respect of the review of group activities can also in general refer to the review following one-to-one interview activities, one of the principal differences being that more time will be necessary because of the greater number of (albeit smaller) 'groups'. However, the questions to be asked will be rather different from those for a group activity and there will be a wider variation between activities because of the more extensive range of interview or interactive situations.

Figure 6.4 is intended to give an indication of an *aide-mémoire* suitable for reviewing in the full group a number of subgroups that have been following the same one-to-one activity. This can be modified according to your special needs.

One-to-One Activity Debrief Aide-Mémoire

Of the interviewer

1. How do you feel that you coped with the situation presented to you?
2. Why do you feel that?
3. What type of structure did you try to apply to the interview?
4. How successful do you feel you were?
5. What problems or problem areas occurred in the interview?
6. How (well) did you deal with these?
7. How did you feel about the behaviours of the interviewee in
   – helping you
   – hindering you?

Of the interviewee

1. How did you feel about your role in the interview?
2. How realistic did you feel the activity was?
3. What problems were caused for you?
4. What were they and how were they handled?
5. To what extent did the interviewer
   – help you
   – hinder you?
6. How well (sympathetically) were you received in the interview by the interviewer?
7. Who suggested the action to be taken?
8. Would you have wanted this in any other way?
9. Was the action agreed really accepted by you?
10. If you had been the interviewer, what would you have done differently?

Figure 6.4 *An interview debrief aide-mémoire*

Final review

After the reviews have been conducted, whether for group or one-to-one activities, a general discussion should be held on the overall learning that has emerged from the activities and the reviews. These should be evaluated against the planned learning objectives and arrangements made for any learning that should have taken place but did not.

USING THE LEARNERS AS EFFECTIVE REVIEWERS

Group activity review

The methods of review described so far involve principally the trainer, as the controller of the event, the questioner of leaders, interviewers, group members, interviewees and observers, and the leader of discussions resulting from this questioning. There can be no doubt that these approaches use the least amount of time possible, particularly when the trainer controls this factor strictly. But they do not necessarily mean that the trainer-led reviews are the most effective. It has been mentioned earlier that more and more learners are looking to take an active role themselves in all aspects concerned with their learning. You should be encouraging this as much as you can, because all indications are that they will accept and learn more if they have had a considerable amount of self-activity. Learning must be more effective if the learners realize themselves what they have done right or wrong, rather than being told by the trainer; even comments from their peers are more likely to be accepted than those from the trainer, however good a relationship has been achieved. It follows therefore that the more involvement the learners have in the review, the more they will be prepared to be open and honest, and to accept the feedback, particularly from their fellow learners.

Approaches using these learner-led techniques can be used for the review of either group or one-to-one activities, both being equally successful. The one-to-one approach has been used for some time and is generally accepted, but the group approach is more radical in its method.

Group, learner-led reviews

This approach requires the use of an observer or observers with each subgroup in a multi-group activity and it is often necessary to increase the number of activities so that all the learners have the opportunity to participate in an activity, and preferably as an observer. The activity proceeds in the normal way, following written briefing of the leader and members and of the observers by the written briefs, their observation instruments and, essentially in this approach, a discussion with the trainer about what is to happen at the end of the activity.

The approach can be summarized as:

1. verbal briefing of the full learner group by the trainer;
2. a period of time allocated for participants to read and digest their activity briefs and role instructions;
3. a discussion between the observers and the trainer including observer brief-reading, observing instrument familiarization and general observer-trainer discussion on approach;
4. the activity performed in subgroups, each with an observer or observers who may look at the group as a whole, or concentrate separately on the leader and/or members;
5. at the end of the activity, a return to the full learning group for comments by the trainer on subsequent action, plus completion of a 'reflection' sheet;
6. return to the subgrouping for review and feedback discussion, observer led and following an effective pattern;
7. return to the full learning group for final review.

Some particular aspects of this approach are:

Stage 3

Stages 1 and 2 are standard approaches, as is part of stage 3. The 'new' part of stage 3 is that you will be describing to the observers what their roles will be after the end of the activity. This is that they will return with the subgroups to the subgroup activity rooms and will lead the review, *within that group*. In effect they will take the place of the trainer, or a trainer that might have been with each subgroup. The advantage is that they too are learners and will themselves be participants in activities at later stages. Consequently, as suggested earlier, they will be accepted more by their peers than perhaps you, as the trainer power figure, would be.

Stage 5

The process of stage 5 is a short summary by the trainer of what is going to happen in the review stage 6, when the review will be conducted by the observers back with the subgroups. The opportunity might be given at this point for anybody to make any significant comment that it is felt should not wait until the subgroup or final reviews.

But the principal activity in this stage will be the opportunity for the participants to reflect on the activity, their part and the parts of others in what happened, and any other thoughts they might have. In many cases the participants might still be on a 'high' or even a 'low' as a result of what happened in the activity. This period of reflection will help them to return to reality and to start thinking about the event in objective terms. In such an atmosphere, where emotions may be high, objective reflection may be difficult if you simply ask them to think about the activity. A useful support for this is to give them a questionnaire on which to answer their reactions to the activity. This summary of their views can be taken with them to the observer-led review and used as an *aide-mémoire* for their comments. Figures 6.5 and 6.6 suggest typical formats for questionnaires of this nature, relying heavily on a scoring scale to concentrate their minds and provide an easy form of comparison in the review. Space (not shown in these figures) should be left between questions for the learners to make notes.

Activity Self-Analysis (leader)

Where relevant, please allocate a score to each of the items, as you saw them, by circling the number you feel best applies to that particular aspect. Add some brief notes to remind yourself of the reason why you have given this score and otherwise add some brief notes. You will be able to refer to this questionnaire in the activity review that follows.

	Good, very or a lot			Poor, not very or not very much		

The Activity and the Task

How successful do you feel you were in achieving the task?	6	5	4	3	2	1
How difficult did you find the task?	6	5	4	3	2	1
How good was the time allocation for the activity?	6	5	4	3	2	1
To what extent did you work to a plan?	6	5	4	3	2	1
Was this plan agreed by all the members?	6	5	4	3	2	1
To what extent did you make use of all the resources at your disposal?	6	5	4	3	2	1
To what extent did you make use of all the information available or obtainable?	6	5	4	3	2	1

What were the major factors involved in the success or failure?

Yourself

How effective do you feel your leadership was?	6	5	4	3	2	1
To what extent did you ensure the members knew what they had to do?	6	5	4	3	2	1
To what extent did you confirm the progress of each member during the activity?	6	5	4	3	2	1
To what extent did you bring everybody in?	6	5	4	3	2	1
How much did you ignore any member?	6	5	4	3	2	1
How often did you summarize progress?	6	5	4	3	2	1
Did you have many problems as a leader?	6	5	4	3	2	1

What were they and how did you overcome
them?
What did you do that helped the process most?
What did you do that hindered the process most?
Was there anything else you could have done to
have helped the activity and the members?
If you had been a member instead of leader,
what would you have done?
If you had to repeat the activity, what changes
would you make?
How would you rate yourself as the leader
in that activity?   6   5   4   3   2   1

The Members

How helpful were your group members
in the achievement of the activity?   6   5   4   3   2   1
How hindering were your group
members in processing the activity?   6   5   4   3   2   1
How did these helps or hindrances show
themselves?
What else would you have liked your
members to have done?
How do you think your members will
score you as the leader?   6   5   4   3   2   1
What have you learned from
the activity that you might be able to
implement on your return to work?

Figure 6.5 *Activity questionnaire (leader)*

Activity Self-Analysis (Group Member)

Where relevant, please allocate a score to each of the items, as you saw them, by circling the
number you feel best applies to that particular aspect. Add some brief notes to remind yourself of the reason why you have given this score and otherwise add some brief notes. You will
be able to refer to this questionnaire in the activity review that follows.

	Good, very or a lot			Poor, not very or not very much		

The Activity and the Task

How successful do you feel you were
in achieving the task?   6   5   4   3   2   1
How difficult did you find the task?   6   5   4   3   2   1
How good was the time allocation for
the activity?   6   5   4   3   2   1
To what extent did you work to a plan?   6   5   4   3   2   1
Was this plan agreed by all the members?   6   5   4   3   2   1
To what extent did the leader make use
of all the resources at your disposal?   6   5   4   3   2   1

| To what extent did the leader make use of all the information available or obtainable? | 6 | 5 | 4 | 3 | 2 | I |

What were the major factors involved in the success or failure?

Yourself

How effective do you feel your participation was?	6	5	4	3	2	I
To what extent did you know what you had to do?	6	5	4	3	2	I
Did you have many problems as a member?	6	5	4	3	2	I

What were they and how did you overcome them?

What did you do that helped the process most?

What did you do that hindered the process most?

Was there anything else you could have done to have helped the activity, the other members and the leader?

If you had been leader instead of a member, what would you have done?

If you had to repeat the activity, what changes would you make?

The Leader

To what extent did the leader confirm the progress of each member during the activity?	6	5	4	3	2	I
To what extent did the leader bring everybody in?	6	5	4	3	2	I
How much did the leader ignore any member?	6	5	4	3	2	I
How often did the leader summarize progress?	6	5	4	3	2	I
How helpful was the leader to the members in the achievement of the activity?	6	5	4	3	2	I
How hindering was the leader in processing the activity?	6	5	4	3	2	I

How did these helps or hindrances show themselves?

What else would you have liked your leader to have done?

| How would you rate the leader in that activity? | 6 | 5 | 4 | 3 | 2 | I |

What have you learned from the activity that you might be able to implement on your return to work?

Figure 6.6 *Activity questionnaire (group member)*

Stage 6

The subgroups and their observer(s) then return to their syndicate rooms for a review, concentrating on the actions of their own sub group. In the 'teach-in' of the observers in stage 3 a common method will have been discussed and agreed. This will be that a sequence of feedback should be followed to ensure that everybody has their say and that every significant aspect of the activity is covered.

There are a number of approaches that have been used in these and similar circumstances, including that of the observer fully taking the place of the trainer and giving the feedback as described at the start of this chapter. But the purpose of this method is to give the participants as much say as possible in the contribution of feedback to themselves and others. So the process I recommend follows the structure that the observer:

1. asks the leader to comment on the activity and about both his or her actions and those of the members;
2. asks the members to comment on both their own and the leader's actions;
3. gives their own comments on both the leader and the members from their observations.

Full use should be made by all participants of their *aide-mémoires* completed at the end of the activity and bare statements should be encouraged to develop into discussions by the observer–leader who in effect becomes a discussion leader. If possible, a summary of the principal conclusions of learning should be produced, perhaps on a flipchart sheet to take back to the main room.

Stage 7

The final stage in this review activity takes place with the full learning group in the main room, sufficient time having been given to them in their observer-led subgroups to discuss as fully as possible all the actions and implications of the activity. Where relevant, the groups will return with flipchart sheets summarizing the learning they have taken from the activity. These can either be exhibited round the room at the same time or one at a time as a spokesperson from each group presents the findings from their group. This can be the observer, but in order to give other participants an opportunity to take an active role a member might be chosen by the group for this task. The trainer usually leads this final feedback discussion, but if the learner-group is a capable one, control can continue in their hands.

The learning points can be discussed by the whole group, particularly if there are significant divergences, and, if there is time, a final, group summary sheet might be constructed for posting on the wall of the main room.

One-to-one activity review

The process of using the observers and learners as the principal reviewers following one-to-one activities is basically the same as that described above for group activities. Each pair of participants during the activity will have an observer and, after the initial recall of all the sub groups to the main room for briefing on the review process, the pairs with their observers can then return to their syndicate rooms for a feedback review, led by the observer. The questionnaires completed at the end of the group activity (Figures 6.5 and 6.6) can be modified for use by the interviewers and the interviewees, using the questions suggested in Figure 6.4.

Video review

If you have been using video recording as part of your observation approaches, you will need to use this in the feedback review. If the learners have been aware of its presence they will expect it to be used and usually are disappointed if it is not. Certainly there would seem to be little point in using it during the observation and not subsequently. The comment has been made earlier that an effective feedback review session requires a substantial amount of time: if video is introduced this time can be extended even more. However, there are a number of ways in which the time can be controlled and the video recording used effectively.

Uses of video in reviews, whether group or one-to-one, can include:

- immediate showing
- leader/interviewer withdrawal
- evening viewing
- post-event use.

Immediate showing

This is the more usual way that the video observation is used, but it is not necessarily the most effective, and can be a major time stealer. If a group activity has been recorded the object of the observation can be the leader of the group or the group members, or both. Usually the recording is intended to show important or significant events or behaviours in the activity, so it would be a misuse of time to show the complete recording. One decision you must make is whether you are going to use the recording alone, or link it with the more traditional verbal review. Including both can use up a considerable amount of time, but you will rarely be able to avoid some verbal review.

Let us take the case of a group activity in which both the leader and the members have been recorded. As the activity has been proceeding, someone (the trainer or other observer) will have been making observation notes and also noting the position in the recording where significant events have taken place. After the activity the video can be preceded by a shortened verbal review of how the leader and the members saw their actions and behaviours, the relevant parts of the video then being shown to make particular or even disputed points. You may feel in certain circumstances that the video can be used alone as the reviewing instrument, but you will find that considerable discussion is generated by even this approach. The essential action, whether or not both approaches are used, is to find quickly on the video recording the place where something that requires discussion can be found. This is not easy to do, and even more time can be used up in searching for parts that may not have had their positions noted – 'It was just after I had said so-and-so to the leader and he had ignored me'!

The full video can be made available to the group for them to view in their own time (for example during the evening), if they so wish. This can be supported, if they really intend to view it, by a period the following morning taking up any further points. There is no doubt that using video in observation and review can use up a considerable period of time. But in many cases this is justified by the visual confirmation of events that may have been queried or disbelieved in a verbal only report. A similar approach can be taken following a one-to-one activity.

Leader/interviewer withdrawal

This is a particularly useful technique in one-to-one activities although it can also be applied to group work. It does, however, require careful planning and timetabling as it involves the withdrawal from the learning event of at least one person, more if several activities have taken place at the same time.

It can be especially timesaving if used when only one or two interviews have taken place at the same time. After the activities, instead of conducting a verbal review, the interviewer withdraws from the event with the video recording to view it in another room, while perhaps further interviews with other learners are taking place. At the end of the next series of interviews the interviewers from these go to view their videos and the first group returns. The principal problem with this approach is when the last series of interviews takes place – the interviewers will only be able to go to view their videos if nothing is to be done with the learning group at this time.

An alternative is for the last group of interviewers to view their videos at the end of the day, thus allowing the training programme to continue. The withdrawal to view the videos can be preceded by a reduced period of verbal feedback, during which the observers suggest areas for the interviewers' particular attention, or the interviewers themselves set objectives based on what they intend to look for. The range of possibilities for this approach is wide, but it can obviously have its problems in terms of discontinuity.

A final alternative is to have a brief verbal review after each interview, with the interviewers being left to view (perhaps with their interviewees) the videos in the evening, a period being set aside the following day to discuss the viewings.

There can be little doubt that video recording of a group or one-to-one activity can give the trainer and the participants material for review that could not be obtained or expressed in any other way. But it will be seen that actually to use it in reviews is fraught with problems of the time taken to review and the availability of the people who wish to review. In addition there is not always the opportunity for a trainer to be present while the video is being viewed so that critical support might be given or queries clarified.

THE END OF THE REVIEW

After the feedback has been given and everybody has had their say (within the time constraints), two actions will complete the review session:

- the production of a final summary of what has been learned from the exercise and the review; and
- commitment from the learners that they will implement at work the learning from the activity and the review.

SECTION TWO

Specific Forms of Activities

7
—

Introductions; Icebreakers; Energizers and Session Shakers; and Buzz Groups

Many of these are the first that most trainers will encounter and, although they are not major events in themselves, their practical importance is much more than their apparent triviality might suggest.

INTRODUCTORY ACTIVITIES

The manner in which an event starts can have a major effect on the rest of the programme – first impressions do count. If a learner has come to an event and is looking forward to a vital, impactive programme, their expectations are likely to subside very quickly if the first part of the event is slow, boring and something they have suffered on every training programme they have attended. The introduction activity can have a considerable influence on these initial attitudes and hence perhaps on subsequent ones.

Description

An introductory activity is one that is intended to start a learning event in the most interesting, informative, useful and enjoyable manner possible. Its objectives are to:

- introduce the learners to the trainer, the training programme and the manner in which it will be conducted;
- introduce the learners to each other and so start a process of relationship building;

■ start the process in which each learner has and takes the opportunity to make a verbal contribution.

Once this process has started, the problems arising from subsequent and continued communication are usually lessened. These problems will not necessarily be eradicated, but where a person's normal behaviour is to sit back and let others speak they are at least given the opportunity and encouraged to speak. They are more likely to continue this participation having started the process of communication with the other members. But an introductory activity does not guarantee continuance unless other activities are quickly brought in.

Membership

The answer to this is simple – everybody should be involved, preferably including the trainers who should encourage openness by being open themselves. Obviously the size of the group, and the type of activity, will have an influence, particularly as everybody is being encouraged to contribute. It would be an unreasonable burden on both the trainers and the learners if everybody in a group of 12 was allowed 15 minutes each – at least three hours would be involved.

Timing

This is obviously linked with the preceding section. The size of the group could, as suggested, be allowed to dictate the time expended but, although the first activity has important ramifications, its relative place in the learning event must be understood. The learners, although accepting the need for intra-introductions, will become impatient to 'get on with the real business' if the introductory activity carries on too long, as they see it. So although it is difficult to put an absolute time on the duration of an activity of this nature in most cases a maximum of an hour should be planned. Some introduction activities, however, merge naturally into the event content, so the timing may become irrelevant – as long as the learners realize the content relevancy.

Planning and design

Two approaches to these activities may be considered. One is where the activity is also linked closely with the content of the learning event; the other is based simply on providing introductions. Part of your event planning must include consideration of which type of introductory activity is going to be most relevant for your event, how long a period should be allocated to it and the programme weighting it should be given. Decisions must also be made about whether the activity should be selected from an existing example or whether attempts should be made to produce an original one. Activities of this nature are common and readily available from a variety of sources, and as they should not occupy too important a role in the event it is doubtful whether too much time and energy should be expended in trying to produce an original.

Availability

Literally hundreds of this general type of activity exist, fewer of the more content specific. The former range from the simplest of introductions 'I am ...' to complex ones in which feelings, views, attitudes and aspirations are disclosed. The latter can include activities which are similar to later activities in the event, but have the introductory objectives as their overriding intent. Many of these objectives have their roots in training programmes that have existed for many years and the established activity collections contain many examples. The major problem, as is the case in the choice of many types of activity, is selecting the most suitable one from the available plethora.

Usage

An introductory activity is naturally held at or near the beginning of a training or learning event, frequently immediately following the 'start' of the event, a start which usually includes a welcome and a statement of the programme 'domestics'. An introductory activity can in fact be included as part of this 'start of programme'.

As has been suggested several times, the number and variation range of introductory activities is large and many examples can be found in the resource literature. One or two are described here.

LET'S ASK THE TRAINER

Immediately after the welcome by the trainer and the identification by name of the trainer (s) present, the learning group is divided into a number of groups of three or four people. The brief given to them for the activity, usually verbally although it can be written on a handout or flipchart sheet, for the activity is to consider what questions they would like to put to the trainer. Subject headings might be suggested, including domestic matters about the training location, training methods to be employed, the specific content of the event, social matters and so on. Different groups might be given one of these subjects to consider or all groups can consider the same questions. A fully open brief might otherwise be given, leaving it completely to the learners to decide what they want to know about. It can be suggested that a member of the group is elected as spokesperson for each group, rather than it be left to chance about how the questions are posed. After ten minutes or so, the groups reconvene into the full group and the questions are posed and answered openly and fully.

You should be careful how you bring the different groups into the questioning. It is easy for one group to take over the period and be the group that asks all the questions; you must ensure that all groups have an equal opportunity to contribute. This will be returned to later.

The advantages of this type of activity include the opportunity for every body to contribute something in the small group, rather than be expected to speak out in the full group (as many individuals may be unwilling to take this step so early in the event). It also gives some members the opportunity to act as public spokespersons and gives anonymity to the originators of the questions which may sometimes be naive, or personal.

THE CREEPING DEATH

There are innumerable versions of this introductory activity, but the classical model is one in which the trainer asks the learners to introduce themselves one after the other, starting at one extremity of, say, a U-shaped seating arrangement and moving round to the other extremity. The trainer can start the process and offer a model for the others to follow.

Variations include briefing the participants about the type of details to give – name, company or branch, job or role, how long in that role, other career details personal details and so on; or they are simply left to decide for themselves what sort and extent of details to give. If the training event is about a specific subject, eg negotiation skills, they can be asked to include information about the extent of their experience in this area, problems encountered in instances in which they have been involved and other views on the subject.

The brief can also include any time constraints thought desirable or necessary – for example no more than three minutes per person, although in practice the full time may not be used. A lot can be said in three minutes, particularly if the speaker knows what they want to say. To help the learners in this time constraint, they can be given, before the actual introductions start, a few minutes to think about and note down what they want to say about themselves. A few minutes expended in this way can save a lot of time later.

The problems associated with this type of approach include the following:

■ Before the speaker has completed introducing themselves, most of the others have stopped listening and are rehearsing what they are going to say – this is reduced somewhat by a pre-activity preparation period, but it is never eliminated.
■ As a result of the ongoing self-rehearsal, listening is either reduced or does not occur at all, so much of what is said can be wasted.
■ Feelings of boredom and concern, even fear, can build up as the participants wait for their turn to speak. Boredom can occur in the ones who can relax because they have made their contribution – they may not stay active by listening to those who follow them; boredom can happen with the ones waiting for their turn to come, particularly those at the end of the line and also if the progress round the group is slow and long winded; and there can be concern/fear about having to speak out in public.
■ Speaking in public can be a very real concern for people with particular dispositions and it can be exacerbated by their having to wait for their turn. I know personally of one man who left the room as it got closer to his turn to speak and in fact he left the course – his was an extreme case as he had medical problems, but unless some warning is given beforehand, all sorts of potential problems can exist in the group and this type of activity might bring them out.

Some of these problems can be reduced by starting the introductions at one end, having two or three learners speak, then moving to the other end for one or two speakers, back to where the first group finished and so on. The most extreme variation is *Russian Roulette* in which you control the order of speaking by selecting the next speaker 'at random'. In this approach it can be very useful to have the obviously nervous ones speak quite early – but not first – in the event. There will, however, always be an obvious ultimate and penultimate speaker whose nervousness may become a problem, but one way of avoiding this might be to select these speakers from participants whom you know are strong characters and who will have no problems.

In spite of all the potential problems the methods described above are still frequently used as they are simple and straightforward, enable everybody to speak and can be controlled to use minimum time.

WHY AM I HERE? OR WHO AM I?

This is a more complex way of obtaining introductions, as here they are linked with a process purpose. The activity is basically a self-mapping one in which the participants are asked to produce a map, drawing or some sort of image about themselves, how they have reached their present stage, what this stage is, what their aspirations might be and so on. The image approach can reduce many verbal requirements, but it shouldn't do this completely otherwise one of the major objectives of having an introductory activity will be lost. There are many variations of this type of activity, some simple, others potentially threatening, and some that can be used effectively even with groups that know each other (or think they do).

One example I have found useful is to ask the participants to write on flipchart sheets comments about certain, defined aspects. The sheets can then be displayed round the walls and the participants give a short presentation explaining their entries. The sheets can be divided into boxes, an example is shown in Figure 7.1.

In the centre circle basic personal details such as name, work location, job role (age, marital status etc) can be entered. In the boxes around the centre, 'A' might be concerned with the problems they have had in the learning area; 'B' what they hope to get out of the event; 'C' how supportive their boss is of their learning; 'D' how they feel about taking part in this event. An alternative might be 'A' – concerns; 'B' – personal strengths; 'C' – expectations of the event; 'D' – boss's expectations; 'E' – personal objectives.

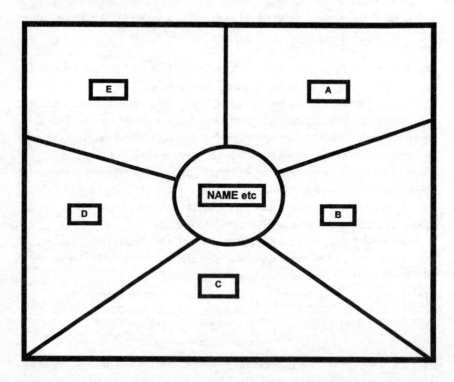

Figure 7.1 *A 'Who am I?' chart*

Introductions with a linked purpose

Some introductory activities have an additional objective, which is to link the objectives of the introductory activity with those of the learning event. A typical example of this might be on an interviewing learning event. Instead of setting up self-introductions, the learning group can be divided into pairs and within the pairs the participants interview each other to bring out the material that would normally be included in a self-introduction, plus, because of the personal approach, information that might not otherwise emerge. In the brief to the activity the participants might also be asked to find out from the person being interviewed their views, experiences, problems etc related to interviewing. The person being interviewed might be asked, in addition to responding to the interviewer's questions, to note the interviewer's style, skill etc. In their pairs, one person interviews the other for up to say eight minutes, then the roles are reversed. A little time may be given at the end of the interviews for the interviewing style observations to be noted and prepared for comment. The second stage in this activity is for one of each of the participants to introduce the person they interviewed, until everybody has been introduced. This can be done by means of the creeping death or one of the other variations.

One major difference with this approach is that, in addition to the participants being introduced rather than self-introducing, there is an opportunity for a review and feedback period, albeit limited at this early stage of the programme. However, it introduces the learners to the concept and practice of review and feedback.

- In this period the interviewees can be asked in the full group to comment on their views of the interviewer's style and how they would otherwise have liked to have been approached.
- Additionally, the 'interviewee' can comment on the quality of the interviewer's introduction of them to the group – its quality, completeness, accuracy and so on.
- As an alternative to the full group review, the pairs can be reconstituted to give each other feedback in their one-to-one environment, rather than in public.

Naturally there are other variations to this approach, some simple, some complex requiring progressive interviewing which can take up a considerable amount of time, but giving everybody the chance to interview everybody else in the group, start building relationships, pass on information and present.

T–CHARTS

T-charts are an alternative to the 'Who am I?' activity shown in Figure 7.1, but are linked more directly with the learning event in addition to letting the learners introduce each other in a specific way. Each learner is given a sheet of A4 paper on which a T has been drawn. The left bar of the 'T' is headed 'Hopes' and the right-hand bar 'Concerns'. This chart is shown in Figure 7.2. The learners are asked to consider their feelings at this early stage of the event, looking forward to it. Under the 'Hopes' part of the chart they are asked to enter their views of what they hope for from the event – what they would like it to do, how they would like it to progress, what they would like to learn, how they feel relationships will develop and so on. On the right-hand side, the 'Concerns', they should enter the doubts they have about the event, and what they really think, rather than hope, will come out of it, in similar terms to the 'Hopes'.

Hopes	Concerns

Figure 7.2 *A T-chart*

A summary flipchart sheet can be produced by the trainer from the calling out by the learners of the entries they have made on their own sheets. Alternatively, they can each come up to a front-of-the-group flipchart sheet and make the entries themselves, avoiding any repetitions. The entries obviously relate to the learning event and when the summary chart is complete, explanations being made where necessary, it can be posted on the wall of the main room. At the end of the event, the chart can be referred to again and the hopes versus the concerns discussed in the light of what has happened during the event.

As has been suggested on several occasions, the number and variation range of introductory activities is large and many examples can be found in the resource literature. Let me complete this section by describing a simple but very effective introductory activity which is one of my favourites. It is particularly useful with a reasonably large group of people who are mainly strangers to each other.

Ask everybody to stand up and go and talk to one other person whom they do not know, for about two minutes. At the end of the two minutes ask them to go and talk to somebody else, and so on for as long as either everybody has met everybody else, or too much time is being taken up. The noise and the fun is tremendous and you can feel the increasing relaxation in the atmosphere. When the time comes to stop the activity, be ready to step in immediately with some other event, preferably an activity to keep the active momentum going.

ICEBREAKERS

Description

Icebreakers are very similar to introductory meetings and merge frequently, particularly as you can describe introductory activities as icebreakers. But the common description of an icebreaker is that it is a short activity, usually engaged in by the whole group, that not only helps the learners to introduce themselves to each other but extends their developing co-relationships to a deeper level. It can also introduce the learners to the learning event in a non-threatening way. In this respect, the interview introductory activity moves a long way along the spectrum towards being an icebreaker.

Membership

All the learners in a learning group are actively involved as in the case of introductory activities.

Timing

Icebreakers can be very short, five minutes is about the shortest practicable, or they can extend for quite long periods, probing deeper into relationships, attitudes and feelings than is possible at the introductory level. Consequently more time is necessary to do this at a safe pace.

Planning and design

Icebreakers can be amalgamated with the introductory activity at the start of the learning event, or follow it immediately. Planning will be determined by the time available and the emotive nature of the event. However, icebreakers can be usefully included when there has been a break in a larger type of programme. For example, I have been involved with a trainers' training and development programme which started with two one-week training events separated by a month to six weeks, the learners continuing their practical projects during this interval. Although by the end of the first week they had come to know each other well, it was felt that something would be necessary at the start of the second week to bridge the gap, prior to having them report on their projects. They had already introduced themselves at the start of the second week, so an icebreaker seemed to be the most relevant 'starter'. There were many examples to choose from, but on this occasion they were asked as part of their interim projects to develop a short icebreaker. The very first activity at the start of their second week was to decide which icebreaker to use. In the end two were selected – one involved the group, in pairs, identifying errors in a large, complex picture produced for this activity, with a prize for the winners; the other was a word-around-the-circle game in which participants had to say particular words, following a set of rules. These were simple activities, little more than party games, but they served their purpose as everybody had a good laugh, enjoyed themselves and were sufficiently relaxed and interrelating well to start the serious business!

Usage and examples

The use of icebreakers at the start of an event or following a break of some nature has been mentioned and in general this icebreaker is a short activity, sometimes humorous and frequently not related to specific training objective or even the programme content.

Usually all the participants on a course welcome these small activities, but care must be taken to ensure that they know what the activities are and why they are being used. There are still learners attending training programmes (usually very strong pragmatists?) who object to playing 'silly little games' because they are not directly related to the learning content. Naturally, if you know you have a group full of these you may think twice about using a non-course related activity. However, this is not an inviolable rule as even the most practical and pragmatic people sometimes enjoy letting their hair down.

ANIMALS

Although the basic use of an icebreaker is simply to do what its name implies, and not necessarily be related to the course objectives, I always prefer them to be more than an incidental game to play. The 'error' and the 'wordspeak' icebreakers mentioned above, although not having in themselves any content learning, were included in a trainer development programme as an icebreaker *and* to give the learner – trainers the experience of constructing and being involved in this type of activity.

Many, if not most icebreakers have an implied objective of deepening a developing relationship in the learning group – if you've played a silly game with the others on the course, you have an immediate bond. 'Animals' is such an activity, although it can be developed considerably in the feedback session that follows it.

■ Have a sizeable set of pictures and drawings (they can be cut-outs from magazines, etc) of a wide range of animals, birds, insects, reptiles and fish, placed in a pile on the floor.
■ Give the individuals five minutes or so to select an animal from the pile that they feel best reflects their personality and behaviour.
■ The selected pictures are given to you by the participants who should be reminded to remember which picture they have chosen.
■ Post the pictures round the walls of the training room.
■ Give the group ten minutes or so to look at the pictures and write down which of the rest of the group chose the various animals.
■ In individual turn, have the group say either:
    which picture they think was chosen by a named individual; or
    which individual chose which picture
    (it will help if you decide in the planning stage which approach
    you will use).
■ Enter the identifications on a flipchart displayed for the group to see – this may show a pattern from the selections.
■ Have each individual disclose (and mark in the final column of the chart) which picture they really chose and why. These choices can then be discussed to whatever depth is found desirable.

In the discussion that follows, if found desirable or relevant at this stage of the programme, comments can be made and sought on how and why people see others differently, often reflecting their own viewpoints. A more advanced discussion can also encourage individuals to say why they identified the particular picture as the one chosen by the individual involved.

INTRODUCTION EXTENSION

This activity can be useful on programmes concerned with developing people in interactive and interpersonal relationship skills and can extend the introductory activity that started the programme. In that initial activity it is rare for information to be given that goes much deeper than the superficial level. This activity encourages a wider emergence of internal views, opinions, feelings and attitudes.

- The activity can be run as a full group activity if it felt that in such a sized group views will be expressed easily and openly, or in small groups if it is felt this will ease personal disclosure. In the latter case you might have a full group session after the small-group discussions to air agreed comments.
- One approach to the activity might be to display a list of subjects from which the participants can chose four or more on which to comment. In the full group approach, part of the activity would be for the group to make their selections as a group; in the subgroup approach each makes their own selections, which may differ from one group to another.
- Subjects to choose from might include:
  My biggest achievement;
  My biggest failure;
  Something I have done that I have regretted ever since;
  What type of person annoys me and why;
  Three people with whom I would most like to talk and why;
  If I had to have *any* different job to the one I have now, what would I choose?
  (For a 'stronger' group) What are my first impressions of the person on my left and how does that person react to these comments? and/or
  What are my first impressions of my fellow learners in this group?
  What additional talents would I like to have?
  What would I do if I knew I had only four weeks to live?
  What would I want people to say about me after my death – what do I think they will actually say?
  What would I do in a definite nuclear three or four-minute warning?
  Three things about me that I didn't include in my introduction (that I wouldn't normally disclose) and why I didn't disclose them;
  and so on.
- The activity should be introduced with the rule that bare statements without full reasons should always be challenged for explanation or clarification.

ENERGIZERS

Description

Energizers, or session shakers as they are sometimes called, are very similar to icebreakers in that they are short, sharp, impactive activities that have no relationship to the programme objectives. The slight difference is that, rather than normally being introduced at the start of a programme or after a major break, they can be inserted at any time. The trigger for their introduction is when the energy level of the group seems to be flagging and something needs to be done to raise this level.

Planning, resources and timing

Because energizers are usually included as additions to the learning programme, they need to be short and usually they are not included in the programme plan. But their *possible* inclusion must be planned for in case the group reaches the level when one has to be injected, and you would be well advised to go into every training programme with a collection of energizers to hand so that you can select an appropriate one if the need arises. As with introductions and icebreakers, energizers abound in the published collections, particularly those of Andy Kirby (1993).

The occasions which you will find most commonly require an energizer include:

- immediately after a heavy midday lunch break – instead of a 'pudding session';
- after a heavy, serious but essential input, when the learners' eyes are seen to be glazing over;
- at the start of the second and subsequent days of an extended training programme – in such cases the learners frequently start to look forward to these inconsequential breaks from serious learning and frequently start demanding them.

Usage

Energizers suffer from the same dangers as icebreakers, so even though one appears to be necessary, it shouldn't be introduced without thought – too frequent a use can have a reverse effect and promote antagonism from the learners. It is a useful approach when you feel an energizer is necessary, to ask the learner whether they would like – beware, however, that their frequent agreement is not just a ploy to avoid the serious business of learning!

Most learning programmes use mental and verbal skills, as do many of the 'practical' activities albeit in a more active form. A useful switch in such circumstances is to use a physical energizer. Similarly, in severely practical programmes, the energizer might be mentally based.

Many party games can be used or adapted as energizers – don't worry about different levels of people thinking that they are childish, some may be but many adults are still children at heart! Some examples of these are as follows.

PAPER CHASE

This is a simple energizer based on a traditional relay activity.

- Form two teams divided into equal halves – as heterogeneous a mix as possible of men and women.
- Place the half teams at opposite ends of the room facing each other.

TEAM A

x x x x x x   x x x x x x

TEAM B

y y y y y y   y y y y y y

- Place a pile of pieces of paper, each with a different word written on them, in front of each half team
- The method of the game is for each member, by hopping on one leg, to cross the room to their other half team; still on one leg, to read the word out to the front member who must say what the word means – the rest of the team can help if the first member cannot describe the meaning
- The recipient member then hops with another piece of paper to the other half team and the process if repeated. The 'hoppers' after they have delivered their paper will then go to the rear of the half team.
- This process is repeated until all the pieces of paper have been delivered and processed.
- The team to deliver the papers first is the winner and should be awarded with a small prize.

Note that:

■ The words on the pieces of paper should not be ones in too common usage, but should be within the knowledge range of the participants – if desired, company or job words might be used.
■ The rules and instructions should be given by the trainer at the start of the activity.
■ There should be a total of about 20 words for each team.

CLOTHES PEGS

I first came across this activity a number of years ago and have re-encountered it in several guises and used in a number of ways, but it has always had basic purposes that are simple in concept, namely energizing, fun, and introducing an element of competition.

■ Divide the group into two groups (the more members a group has the better as they will probably get in each others' way and cause some panic).
■ Give each group a stable table and a number of wooden or plastic clothes pegs (the spring variety) – about 100 pegs for each group should be sufficient.
■ The groups are given five minutes to build a peg tower, as tall as possible, and stable enough only to stand long enough to be measured.
■ Immediately at the end of the five minutes, stop the building and eithe:r
  – the trainer(s) measure the towers; or
  – each team uses the tape measure it has been give to measure the height of the other team's tower (be prepared for accusations of incorrect measuring or knocking down the tower!);or
  – each team measures its own tower.

This is one of the few energizers that can be repeated during the same programme, the repetition increasing the competitiveness and the 'fun' content.

'MENTAL' ACTIVITIES FOR PRACTICAL TRAINING GROUPS

I have found three useful and acceptable energizers for this type of learning group:

- Charades – one or two only by teams in competition on each occasion the energizer is used;
- Dingbats – again one or two only, with teams in competition;

(these two can be repeated in a longer programme with different examples but the same teams)

- A written, general knowledge quiz (some of these can have hidden twists).

BUZZ GROUPS

Description

Buzz groups are usually more informal and less structured than even introductory activities, icebreakers and energizers and can be introduced at any time in a learning programme from the very start to the end. They are usually impromptu divisions of the learning group into small groups to discuss something that may have arisen by accident or design. The 'buzz' comes from having a number of small groups together in the one room, all talking at the same time to an observer the room would seem to buzz.

Membership

Again, everybody in the learning group is actively involved, but in subgroups. The size of the buzz groups will depend on the size of the main group: with a main group of 12, the usual division would be into four groups of three – three is sufficiently small to encourage each member to have their say, but large enough to offer different points of view. With larger groups than 12, either there can be more buzz groups or larger membership of each group. I have used this method with a group of 100+ when I asked them to form groups of eight or nine members. This seemed to work well.

Timing

Buzz groups are usually formed for quick deliberation, discussion or identification, so usually their lifetimes are short – ten minutes is a common period of time. As suggested above, they can be used at almost any point in an event where their use would seem to be beneficial.

Planning, design and usage

Although many buzz groups are spontaneous events, they can be planned as part of the programme in a structured way. The introduction activity is an example of this where it was decided before the programme to start it in this way. With very large groups I have used this in a planned way to control the post-talk question and answer session, because of the numbers involved and the frequent difficulties of questions in an audience of this size; or you may decide at some point in an input session to change the general passivity of the session and form buzz groups to consider their views on a point that has just been made. Frequently, during an input session, rather than the trainer delivering a list of qualities or the like, the group can be divided into buzz groups to produce their own lists.

Buzz groups are little different from activities in which subgroups are sent away to consider a topic and report back at the end of their discussions, except that the buzz groups stay in the room and usually are considering a more restricted topic.

The practice is simple and involves suggesting that the learning group form threes by moving their chairs together to form their little buzz group, separated from the other threes often only by the simple action of the chair movement. Larger groups need to move their chairs to different parts of the room to form their buzz groups, perhaps in a discussion circle. Sometimes this produces practical, but not insurmountable difficulties: the seats may be fixed to the floor. In such a case the seats are usually in rows so part of one row can simply swivel in their seats to face part of the row behind to form the buzz groups.

The objectives for buzz groups, as with the division of almost any larger group into smaller groups are to:

- add variety to a session;
- encourage the learners to discuss;
- give quieter members the opportunity to speak in a small group;
- enable a variety of views to emerge;
- obtain a large number of views etc in a short time;

- enable the learners to learn from each other;
- help learners gain knowledge in a very safe environment;
- preserve the anonymity of the views of the group members.

The latter objective can be controlled by one of the group being elected to speak for the group, reporting the group's views rather than an individual's views, even though this individual's views do not represent those of all the group.

The subjects for buzz groups can include:

- producing questions in an introduction activity;
- producing views in an end-of-event, closing session;
- producing lists of relevant items during a session – for example, in response to a question from the trainer 'What are the main barriers to verbal communication between people?';
- producing ideas for action in a problem-solving situation.

Reviewing

As the buzz group approach is usually simple, the review application will be equally simple, though even here one or two guidelines can be helpful:

- When you call a halt, it is often useful to allow the learners to stay where they have been buzzing – this encourages each member to relate to what their spokesperson is saying.
- Ask the spokesperson to report then invite the other members of the buzz group to add anything omitted – they are unlikely to do so, but you should still make the offer.
- Ensure that every buzz group has the opportunity to contribute.
- If a number of issues have been discussed, ask each group in turn to comment, avoiding repetition. For the next round of reporting, change the order of the buzz groups in speaking to avoid a repetitive 'creeping death'.
- Encourage the groups to challenge each other's views – this can often result in a useful building on the original statement.
- Wherever possible, write up the groups' views on a flipchart – this will demonstrate that you are listening and that what they are saying is sufficiently important to record.
- Don't be afraid to intervene if one group seems to be going to make all the contributions in one go and thus leave the others nothing to say – if you allow this it could give the impression to the non-contributing groups that they need not bother during a later buzz group.

■ Linked to the last item, if you hold a number of buzz groups, mix the groups differently on each occasion to ensure a wide sharing of views and group familiarization.

A final caveat for the activities just discussed – introductory activities, icebreakers, energizers and buzz groups – must be not to overuse them, because of the potential danger of some learners rejecting them as irrelevant and time wasting. Even if only one or two learners feel this way their discontent can spread only too readily to the remainder of the group, particularly if they are a very vocal minority. As far as possible, you should *plan* their inclusion and identify sections of the programme when an energizer is most likely to be needed. Remember also that more structured and content-oriented activities can often serve as energizers without the danger of criticism of non-relevancy.

Reference

A Compendium of Icebreakers, Energizers and Introductions (1993) Kirby, Andy (ed), Gower.

8

—

Question and Answer; Group Discussions

QUESTION AND ANSWER

Description

The question and answer (Q and A) approach must be one of the most fundamental of the participative methods used in training and development, but it is one that must be used with considerable care. If not used with care it can become a cross-examination or a very formal trainer to member–member to trainer culture rather than a desirable trainer–member–member–member pattern. What must be avoided is the pattern of interaction shown in Figure 8.1 it should be developed into that shown in Figure 8.2.

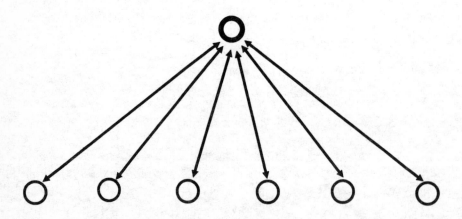

Figure 8.1 *Trainer–member question and answer pattern*

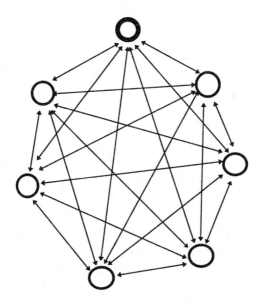

Figure 8.2 *Member-trainer-member-member question and answer pattern*

Planning and design

Although questions can be posed by the trainer at any time, if you intend to use them quite extensively you would be well advised to plan your approach as carefully as the remainder of your session. You will have to decide on whether you will use question and answer, the extent to which you will use the technique and in which parts of the session.

In addition you will have to decide on the relevancy of question and answer – there is little sense in asking questions if the subject is so completely new to the group that they cannot be expected to have any views about it – silence, and deservedly so, will be the result of questions in such circumstances.

Finally, you will need to decide on the extent and content of your questions or the responses you hope to receive. Both you and the learners will soon tire of your having to say, when they do respond with something, 'No, that's not quite what I was looking for.'

The principal occasions on which you will use the Q and A approach will include:

- confirming that the group is keeping up with the learning progress;
- checking the learners' level of knowledge;
- obtaining information from the learners rather than your giving it;

- helping to start a discussion;
- determining the group's awareness in the situation;
- helping the learners to work out the learning for themselves.

Questioning techniques

Most Q and A sessions that fail, whether they are learning methods in their own right or part of another activity, input session or review, do so because of the way in which the questions are asked. A question receives the answer that it deserves in terms of how it is posed – a badly posed question deserves a poor answer.

All questioning should follow a pattern of moving from areas where the material is known, through areas in which the learner will have to reflect and consider before responding, to the more testing areas where the learner will have to use prior learning and reasoning to be able to respond. Problems can easily arise if the questioning jumps straight into the final stage. This approach corresponds to the basic training technique of moving from the known to the unknown.

One basic element of questioning that you must bear in mind when posing your questions to the learners is that, unless unusual circumstances dictate, you should not allow a bare statement to remain unclarified – you may not have the opportunity to return to it later – nor a statement of disagreement, without the reasons being given, to remain unchallenged. In the latter case you must make it clear that you are not challenging the person or their right to disagree, but their failure to back this up with reasons or argument. The more the learners have to express their views specifically and consequently have to think harder about them, the more both they and the other participants are likely to learn.

Another basic element you should always bear in mind when questioning a group of learners is that most people need time to think when asked a question, and a particularly probing question will almost certainly be met by silence while the learners consider what they know or feel in relation to the question. Beware the immediate answer which may be only a facile, superficial response. Inexperienced trainers particularly fear silence when they have asked a question, and tend to panic if the answer is not quickly forthcoming. As a result they jump in with another question which has the effect of confusing the learners and causing even further silence.

One of the other major reasons why silences may follow your questions is that you have made the question so unclear that the learners do not know how to respond. If you receive a longer than expected silence (and make sure that it really is long – in such circumstances seconds seem to be as long as minutes), ask yourself whether you posed your question in a clear, understandable form. You may then need to ask if the question was understood or, perhaps more appropriately, rephrase and repose the question in a more appropriate form.

The questioning maxim should be 'When you have posed a clear, understandable question – wait'.

Types of questions

You should always consider two aspects of questioning – what questions you are going to ask and how you are going to pose them. The first aspect should be part of your session planning and be concerned with the content of the event. The second should eventually be part of your unconsciously applied skills of questioning, although in your possibly inexperienced stage you may have to be very conscious of what you are saying.

The content of your questions should follow some simple rules:

- Do not pose questions to catch the learners out or belittle them.
- Ask questions that you know they should be able to answer, albeit at times with difficulty.
- Relate the questions to the area being studied and only include ones about future material if you do not know the extent of their knowledge of this material.

Appropriate questions

The way in which you ask your questions will determine to a large extent the quality and quantity of the responses. To ensure that you obtain the maximum response in both respects remember there are ways of questioning that are more and less appropriate. Note that I do not say 'appropriate' and 'inappropriate' or 'right' and 'wrong', as even 'wrong' questions can be 'right' on certain occasions.

- *Open or broad-based questions.* These are questions that are intended to elicit as much information etc as possible without the need for further questions at the basic level. They encourage the responder to give extended or similarly 'open' answers, usually with some thought having been given to the answer. Many of these questions start with What, To what extent, How, How much, When, Who, Who else, Where and Why. If you are finding it difficult to ask open questions, try starting them with these words. Open questions are often the best way to start a questioning session and a typical example might be 'We're going to look at x. To what extent have you been involved in this type of work?'

- *Probing questions*. These are the questions that set out to extend the limited information that might have been given in response to one of your questions, such as the last-mentioned above. Questions of this nature can be phrased 'You said that... Can you tell us more about that?' or simply 'Tell me more about that'. Again the more open approach, rather than specific, direct questions, is used to encourage the responder to expand on the amount of information or feelings given.

- *Clarifying questions*. These are similar to probing questions in that they are used where the initial or even subsequent response is not sufficiently extensive or clear to enable you to fully understand what has been said. A clarifying question such as 'What exactly did you mean when you said...?' should produce a response that will clear up any confusion.

- *Testing understanding*. There are three reasons for posing this type of question. One seeks to ensure that the learners have understood what you have said; another sets out to confirm your understanding of a response given to one of your questions or to a statement made by a learner; and the third is intended to help the responder ensure that they are saying what they have meant to express.

   As with the probing and clarifying questions, testing understanding will not only help you and the individual responder, but also the rest of the group who may be having similar problems.

Less appropriate questions

These are questions that under normal circumstances should not be asked, although this is too extreme a stricture as they can be used appropriately in certain situations.

- *Closed questions*. Closed questions are those that require, or produce, either 'Yes' or 'No' as the response, or short answers that give away little information. The response to a question such as 'Did you come this morning' will usually produce 'Yes' or 'No', and to the question 'In which year did you pass your driving test?' the response might be something like a bare '1984'. The result of a closed answer to a closed question is usually that you are forced to think of another question to ask, whereas more extensive information might have been obtained in the first place with an open question.

- *Leading questions*. These give the potential responder information about the type of answer you are seeking. For example, 'Don't you agree that we should do...?' will usually bring a response of agreement, particularly if the responders want to ingratiate themselves with you, even if they disagree. Consequently you may not be receiving an honest response.

■ *Multiple questions.* The problem about asking a composite question that includes a number of questions is that you are unlikely to receive an answer to all the parts, just the ones the individual
  – wants to answer;
  – knows the answer to;
  – can remember from the question.

Whichever the reason, you have wasted a lot of your question and will have to ask further questions.

■ *Hypothetical questions.* These questions pose situations that are hypothetical, not real. They deserve, and usually receive, hypothetical and unreal answers. Questions should be related to real issues as there can be no justification for the unreality of a hypothetical answer.

Other types of questions include:

■ *Reflections.* These are not actually questions but statements that serve the same purpose as questions. They are a method of encouraging a hesitant or reluctant speaker to say more than the brief comments they may have made. Some people do not respond well to questioning, but if reflections are used skilfully they do not realize they are being probed and respond quite readily. If a learner has made a limited response and you require more, but realize that to question might make the person close up, you might say something like 'What you seem to be saying is that there is a problem.' Note that this is not said in the form of a question, but simply a restatement of what the person has said. Most people, realizing (perhaps subconsciously) that you are sympathizing with them, would respond to this with 'Yes, you're right. I seem to be having a problem with... and this is causing me...' carrying on to extend the information they can give. Carried out skilfully, people will not be aware that reflecting is taking place and will open up naturally.

■ *Too simple questioning.* Learning groups will be very suspicious of questions that appear too simple. Their reactions could be:
  – the trainer is insulting their intelligence and skill;
  – the trainer is out of touch with their capabilities;
  – there's a catch in the question!

Ensure that your questions are sufficiently demanding to avoid these accusations, stated or not, but be careful not to swing too far the other way and make the questions impossibly difficult.

■ *Too difficult questioning.* These may give the learners the false impression that they should know the answers and therefore make them feel inadequate. What it really means is that the trainer has not researched and planned sufficiently well to get the level of the questioning appropriate.

Problems in questioning

Posing both the appropriate and *type* of question are not the only problems you might encounter in a Q and A session or part of a session. Some of these, eg silences, have already been mentioned but there are others.

■ *Nominating the responder.* This is always a difficult problem and sometimes I feel too much is made of it. The advice usually given is not to direct a question to an individual by name (sometimes referred to as 'naming the victim') as this might make them feel that undue pressure is being put on them or, worse, it is assumed that they do not know the answer and are being picked on. This may in some circumstances be the case, but it is far from the general situation. If you want to avoid the problem ask the question without naming anyone, but looking at the person you want to respond. However, they might not do so and you are still left with the problem. If someone constantly avoids answering, then there is justification in asking them directly and by name as this is probably the only way you will get them to answer! As suggested, I suspect that naming the person at whom the question is aimed causes a lot less damage than is usually thought, though if the person described never answers a question voluntarily, how are you to know whether they are learning or not? This has a damaging effect on the training you are offering.

■ *The constant responder.* Every group has its high contributor/high reactor (usually more than one) who can always be relied on to make a response when the trainer poses a question. Often these are valid contributions, but unfortunately the more they talk the less opportunity the quieter members have to speak. Some, in fact, use this as a shield to help them avoid speaking! Apart from the very directive approach of telling them to shut up (perhaps the final option) or having a quiet word with them outside the training and asking them to help you to bring in the quieter members (the usual advice given), they can be controlled in other ways.

Even if they give you a full answer (again) to one of your questions, thank them, but then immediately go to one of the quieter members and say something like 'Fred says... How do you feel about that? Have you had any experience of that? What would you do in this case?'. You may only get back confirmation that they agree with Fred, but at least someone else has spoken and you may be able to go back to them with a probing question. The next time Fred (or Mary) jumps in with an answer before anyone else, repeat the process: they will soon realize what is happening and hopefully will voluntarily start to reduce their contributions. If this doesn't work, you still have the option of telling them to shut up or having a quiet word with them!

- *The reflected question*. It is not unknown for a learner to respond to a question from the trainer by saying 'But what do you think?'. This can frequently happen in certain circumstances, but whatever the situation you should still try to get the group to answer rather than give your own views. After all, the purpose of the questioning was to help them to learn and this would be less if you did all the commenting. Often this situation has been preceded by the trainer always putting questions from the a learner back by saying 'What does the group think? This can become annoying to a learning group after a time.

    It is not easy to give general advice, but you can always say that although you could *tell* them, would they not agree that the learning will be stronger if they worked things out for themselves – a useful leading question!

- *Disagreement*. Some trainers panic if, after raising questions, there is disagreement among the members of the group and this is demonstrated in a very lively discussion. Rather you should welcome this to some extent, as it demonstrates that you have raised interest among the members (one of the objectives of training!). Your role in this situation is to help to control the discussion from becoming too emotive and avoid conflict as opposed to disagreement. You can help to do this by intervening when disagreements are raised without reasons being given – having to give the reasons often cools the atmosphere and the discussion can be brought back to a rational level. Finally, you should try to bring the conflict to a conclusion, whether this is a resolution of the divergent views or an agreement to disagree on the basis that different people are entitled to differing views.

General guidelines

- Listen carefully to every response, especially for any disguised questions or uncertainty within the response.

- Acknowledge every response in some way.
- Show non-verbally (nods, smiles, eye contact) that you are listening.
- Don't reject a response out of hand – at least the individual has bothered to respond with what is their view.
- Don't accept incomplete or unclear answers – ask a clarifying question. Remember that by doing this you may be helping the other members who may also not have understood.
- Try to obtain the views of as many learners as possible, especially the quiet ones.
- Where relevant, eg obtaining a list of qualities, write the answers on a flipchart sheet, using as closely as possible the contributors' own words and not ignoring any valid points.
- Always be honest with the learners. Remember a Q and A session should work both ways. If you are justifiably asked a question, give an honest and open answer or promise to find out (and do so as soon as you can).
- Don't be 'mirror-man' and always be throwing questions put to you back to the group with 'What does the group think?' sometimes someone in the group will have the information required if it is a request for information, but don't just throw questions back at them for the sake of doing so.

GROUP DISCUSSION

Description

Discussions are the natural extensions to question and answer approaches and can be defined as conversations with a purpose, conversations in which a group, whether of two or more, explore a topic. The boundary between conversations and discussions is vague, but the latter are usually more formalized and frequently have a leader.

Discussions in training and development programmes can be either spontaneous, in which case the discussion arises unprompted and is allowed or encouraged to continue by the trainer, or is a pre-planned exercise. Many structured group activities, case studies and simulations contain discussions, although these are usually the means to an end rather than the principal activity itself. These included discussions are in effect pre-planned – the intention of the activity being to produce a result by the group discussing the problem. But other pre-planning can be more directive towards discussion. Prior to the training programme, the trainer will have decided that at point 'x' in a session, in order to involve the learners, to have their views emerge, or simply to break the pattern of the session, a discussion will be started. In such cases the trainer, although not appearing to do so, will control the activity.

Membership

In the majority of cases all the learners will have the opportunity to take part in the discussion, as there will normally be no observers. But, particularly if the group is larger than about six people, there is every likelihood that not everybody will have the chance to have their say. Of course, in any discussion of a particular topic not everybody will have sufficient knowledge to make an original contribution, but everybody can be involved by inviting the non-contributors to consider a point that has been made and from their new viewpoint say what they think about it.

In any case you, as the leader of the discussion, must always be aware of the contribution pattern of the group and be ready to involve those who for any reason are not contributing. One approach to increasing this awareness, particularly in the early stages of a programme, is to have a colleague, as quietly and as inconspicuously as possible, observe the group using behaviour analysis. Although an open approach is to let the group know what is being done, making them aware too early in the programme that they are under observation can make them modify their behaviour to the extent that it becomes unnatural, and the exercise is defeated.

Timing

At the risk of repetition, the length of time taken by the discussion will depend on:

- the importance of the subject;
- any time allocation;
- any time period allotted to discussion.

You have a greater ability to control this time if the discussion has been pre-planned – you know the extent of the subject and will have a reasonable idea of the likely extent of contributions from the learners. Spontaneous, unplanned discussion is more dangerous, and you will need to keep a close check on the use of time. It may be that the points you were going to make in a different manner emerge in the discussion, so you can afford to allow it to extend; or that the topic has taken on an importance with the learners and their programme that you feel that time should be given to it at the expense of other planned aspects.

But in many cases spontaneous discussions have a habit of simply carrying on, and if uncontrolled by the trainer will eat excessively into the time available. One gambit may be to *suspend* the discussion by suggesting that this is a topic that can either be taken up at a later stage or that the learners may wish to continue to discuss after the training periods.

Planning and design

The objectives of a discussion can have a very wide range and can include:

- encouraging the sharing of information among the members and with the trainer;
- encouraging the sharing of personal experiences;
- encouraging the sharing of views, attitudes and feelings about a particular topic;
- applying a particular learning topic or discussing its manner of application;
- deciding on the forward progress of the learning;
- completing problem-solving and decision-making on programme or skill-related issues;
- continuing training in a different way to the existing technique, eg input sessions or practical activities.

Linked with these objectives the discussions must have a number of intents which will include:

- involving all learners in the discussions, particularly the quieter ones;
- having an effect on the individual and group attitudes of the members;
- enabling individual conclusions to be drawn and tested.

Spontaneous discussions neither require nor are capable of any preparatory work, although you will need to make up your mind, either in advance of the training or when you become aware of the learning group and how it is progressing, whether you will allow or even encourage spontaneous discussion during the event. If time for the programme is strictly limited, and spontaneous discussion would endanger its success, you may wish to let the learners know at an early stage the rules relating to this, perhaps suggesting on a residential event that they may wish to hold informal discussions during the evening, or even that you would be prepared to offer voluntary, more informal, discussion sessions in the evening.

Planned discussions require a significant amount of preparation, and a summary of these actions is:

1. Decide on the topic – which can be a subject in itself or one which would be part of a larger subject coverage.
2. Decide how to launch the discussion:
   - a reference to previous material;
   - a provocative statement;
   - an extension of the current input;
   - showing a visual aid containing a statement or statement graphic.
3. Decide on and write down your opening statement or quotation – the starter is often the most difficult so if it is written down and perhaps memorized, this is something less for you to have on your mind as you get started
4. Decide on the seating if this is feasible – a circular arrangement is usually found to be be the most effective. Make the seating change, if this is necessary, a natural event, rather than for example moving the seats when the group is out of the room: this can make them suspicious and less likely to discuss.
5. Decide on your own role – preferably initiator and prompter during the discussion, although you may be asked or required to take a more active role. In general, having introduced the subject and perhaps given a trigger to start the discussion, your role should be unobtrusive and neutral, expressing your own views only if pressed to do so, or if required by the discussion. The discussion is usually held to obtain the views of the members, not yours.
6. Identify any special actions you may need to take. You may know that the group will find it difficult to maintain a discussion – keep one or two ideas or statements ready to throw into the discussion if it starts to flag. You may know that certain members will try to dominate the discussion – decide how you will try to control these.
7. Decide whether you are going to challenge incomplete or unclear contributions yourself or are going to leave this to the members themselves, bringing out what happened in the subsequent review, particularly if the challenges were not made. How can you encourage these inter-member challenges during the discussion?

THE DISCUSSION-LEADING BRIEF

You will need some form of discussion-leading brief in the same way that an input session or presentation brief is essential. This will obviously be not as extensive as the presentation brief, but will serve the same purpose – it will remind you of the topics that should be/must be covered during the discussion if it is to be comprehensive and as valuable a learning vehicle as possible. There are two main forms of brief:

- the shopping list
- the pros and cons list.

Which one you use will depend on your own personal preferences and also on the complexity of the subject to be discussed.

The shopping list

This is a simple reminder list, laid out in whichever format suits you best (vertical, horizontal, patterned). It includes key words that will remind you of the subjects that should be discussed during the event – the training technique of 'must knows, should knows and could knows' can be very useful here. As the discussion progresses, the items satisfactorily covered can be struck off the list, the remainder acting as a reminder of what else should be discussed. This is particularly useful when the discussion falters and subjects from the 'remainder' part of the list can be raised with the group.

The pros and cons list

When you consider as a possibility or know that the subject to be discussed will arouse controversy and/or will be complex, with different members taking differing and opposing views, a pros and cons list can be produced prior to the discussion. This will include in a summarized form, as many of the subject aspects and arguments that you are able to identify.

Divide an A4 sheet of paper vertically as shown in Figure 8.3. Head the left column 'Pros' and the right column 'Cons' and list as many of the aspects and arguments as you can in their relevant columns. During the discussion, as with the shopping list, strike through subjects covered effectively and use the remainder, not only as simple reminders of

PROs	CONs

Figure 8.3 *A pros and cons list*

subjects to be covered, but also a checklist of the main arguments that should emerge.

Both these approaches should help you to keep track of the progress of the discussion and ensure that all the significant topics have been covered to the necessary extent .

Usage And Methods

Introducing the discussion

The method of introduction will have a considerable impact on the success and effectiveness of the discussion, a poor start discouraging the members from opening up and giving their views. The introduction of the discussion has already been commented on, when it was suggested that you should decide on and write down your opening statement or quotation. An impactive opening can often help a discussion along, but don't make it too gimmicky.

One or two examples may illustrate what I mean by an impactive opening – one more impactive than the other.

A DISCUSSION ON DIVORCE AND RELATED ITEMS

This opening involves a sheet of flipchart paper on which is written '2 out of 3'. The group is then asked to say what they think this reference is about. If the required answer is not forthcoming, add 'Marriages'; this may produce the required comment. If not, complete the statement by 'end in divorce' and start the discussion by asking the group for their views on this. The introduction as shown both starts the discussion in a different way and also provides a flipchart sheet that can be posted at the front of the group as a reminder of the subject being discussed.

THE EXPLOSION

One presentation that I shall never forget was set up as a discussion on safety. The presenter was an explosives expert who, having introduced himself, started his presentation. Immediately there was an explosion from the back of the room which, to say the least startled everybody – fortunately nobody had a heart condition! The presenter said, when peace had been restored, 'That was an explosion caused by "x" [an infinitesimal amount of a certain explosive]. You will be able to imagine what "y pounds" will do!' We were aware, alert and eager to say something – even out of sheer fright, and the discussion started without anyone realizing it. Perhaps an overly dramatic opening but it certainly started the proceedings 'with a bang'.

THE 'BAD' DISCUSION

Where the learners have little knowledge or experience of discussion leading or work, the obvious starting point is some form of input or presentation about techniques and methods. But this can be reduced to a large extent by a discussion 'activity' which sets out to raise many of the aspects found in discussions, particularly in bad ones.

- You can announce that you intend to hold a short discussion to start the learning about the subject and seek one or two volunteers. Immediately nominate up to six of the learners to bring their chairs forward and form a circle. It will help if you can include at least one person whom you know will say little or nothing and at least one person whom nothing will stop contributing and probably interrupting. You may sometimes be able to enlist the help of an ally who will take on a role.
- Tell the 'discussion' group that they are going to discuss a subject and ask them to suggest a topic. Allow one or two suggestions to be made, then state that the subject of the discussion will be 'x', a subject decided by you and which you know the members will know something about, but not too much.
- Start the discussion by going on at length with your own opinions, and not allowing the members to interrupt you until you are ready to stop. Then invite the members to contribute and as they do so, interrupt whenever

you feel disposed to do so, usually to flatly disagree or state your views, particularly if the contributor you interrupt is the high contributor. Do not invite the quiet person to say anything and interrupt them if they choose to do so. Exercise little control over the discussion. If a member has been reasonably withdrawn, ask them directly and by name what they think, particularly if the area of discussion at that time is not clear.

- At the end of about ten minutes, or sooner if the discussion has come to a halt (make little attempt to keep it going, other than perhaps to restate your views) state bluntly that that is the end of the discussion and send the members back to their places.
- While this 'discussion' has been proceeding the remainder of the group will have been observing, either without a brief or simply having been asked to watch out for the various actions and behaviours in the discussion.
- When everybody has resumed their places commence a review, first asking the 'observer' group to comment on what they saw, then bringing in the 'discussion' group for their reactions. The review can be completed by a posted summary on a flipchart sheet of the learning points that emerged from the discussion and the review. This summary will make a major input unnecessary as many of the points will have emerged – and through activity the learning will be of a high level.

The objectives for an activity of this nature will include:
- the need to maintain the discussion in an acceptable manner;
- the leader not to state his or her own opinions, particularly at the start of the discussion;
- the interests of the members not being ignored;
- controlling the members' behaviour in a supportive rather than negative way;
- ensuring that all members contribute and the balance is fairly equal;
- that interruptive behaviour, either by the leader or a member, can be disruptive;
- that a non-contributing member if not brought in will frequently remain silent and be almost as much a danger to the discussion as the 'loud' member.

During the discussion

After the introduction, the biggest danger for the leader is jumping in and delivering a monologue of their own views. This is particularly the case for the less experienced leader who, having introduced the subject, in the same way that we found with the trainer posing questions, finds that there is no immediate response. Sit out the silence – provided you have made the subject clear and posed a positive question, the members are probably thinking out their views before speaking.

In the same way, during the discussion, a silence does not necessarily mean that there is nothing to be said. Leave the group to decide whether they have anything further to say, and if you assess that the silence is continuing for longer than you would expect under these circumstances, question the group about whether they have any further views, or perhaps throw in another aspect of the subject from your shopping list.

Your major role will be to:

- sit back and listen once you have started the discussion among the members;
- take notes for later reference – task progress and discussion process;
- check off your shopping list for coverage of the subject;
- intervene only when essential:
  - too much interrupting;
  - the start of active conflict;
  - unchallenged major or unclear statements;
  - to bring-in non-contributors, but in a tactful way;
  - if misinformation is going to mislead the members or disrupt the discussion;
  - giving your own views if requested, or unsolicited if there has been an agreement that you should do so;
  - refreshing a flagging discussion by bringing-in items from your shopping list and seeking the group's views;
  - to suggest that the subject be considered from other viewpoints that have not been covered.

These and other situations suggest that the leader might be taking a major interventionist role, however this would only be necessary when the discussion wasn't working well. If, having introduced the subject and started the discussion, there seem to be few process problems, the interventions should only be made as a last resort. Depending on the objectives or nature of the discussion it may be more appropriate for learning if notes are made of group wanderings for feedback in the review period.

Ending the discussion

Discussion activities of the pre-planned type are usually allocated a period of time within the learning programme and you, acting as leader of the discussion, will need to stop the discussion at the required time or otherwise decide to allow it to continue if:

- the group is learning a lot from the experience, more than would be learned from any subsequent action;
- extension would not interfere with any planned subsequent activities.

Of course, the discussion might end before the allocated time if the group covered the subject successfully in the shorter time. In this case no attempt should be made to extend the discussion simply for the sake of filling the time – more will be lost by this than by accepting the situation and moving on.

Summaries

Before the discussion session ends completely, what has happened during the discussion and what might have been agreed or proposed should be summarized. Options here include the summary being made by the leader (trainer) or, preferably, having the learners summarize the discussion results themselves. You can supplement this summary when they have finished with items they may have omitted and which it is essential to include.

If there have been observers to the discussion a useful variation is to have the observers provide the summary initially, supplemented or modified by the discussion members and, if necessary (usually not!) by you. It can often be very interesting and informative when the views of the observers and the participants diverge because of different viewpoints.

If the discussion activity continues over a long period of time, is particularly complex or covers a number of topics interim summaries are useful, the final summary being in effect a 'summary of the summaries'. Caveats to be observed at the end of the discussion when it is being summarized include:

- ensure that the summary is complete and above all accurate;
- summarize what was said or agreed, not what you/they would have liked to have been said or agreed;
- make sure that agreements are such – that is, agreed by all – otherwise identify any agreements that are still not fully agreed by all members;
- do not include in the summary items that did not arise during the discussion;
- do not use the summary, if it is being made by you, to launch into a teaching session or to raise new issues.

9
—

Structured Group Activities

DESCRIPTION

It is very difficult to produce a clear and comprehensive description of this group of activities as not only is its range very wide, but there is no standard and accepted set of words to name them. The names range from simply 'activities', through 'syndicate exercises or activities', 'games' and so on. There are more specialized and easier to describe 'activities' – eg case studies, simulations, outdoor activities, brainstorming – and some of these will be described in later chapters.

Basically a structured group activity is the next step up from the buzz group described in Chapter 7, but instead of taking place almost informally in the training room the learning group is usually divided into subgroups who retire to separate rooms to perform the activity, returning to the main room, for at least some period, to review the activity performance. It consists of some form of activity – a very wide term – performed in these circumstances, generally for specific learning or learning support purposes. The emphasis is on people doing things in large or small groups rather than as individuals and in a more passive mode.

Forms of activities

There are three major forms of such activities. One is completely artificial, being a constructed activity, eg a problem-solving exercise, which has no relationship to the work of the learning group, or even to work itself, for example the classical NASA activity in which a group is assumed to have crashlanded on the moon with a selection of effects. The problem to be solved is the prioritization of these articles in such a survival situation.

The second is an activity in which, eg the problem to be solved is an actual work one, either one that has already been solved and the group's approach can be weighed against the real-life decision, or one which is current and for which no solution has yet been found. An interim type of activity of this nature would be one in which a hypothetical but real work problem that has not yet arisen would be posed, within the limits of the learning to that stage, for the group's decision.

The third type is again artificial, and one which has no immediate relationship to the work culture or environment, but the lessons to be drawn from the activity and the way in which the solution is approached are totally applicable to the working situation, linked of course to the event objectives. The NASA activity quoted above can be extended to become an example of this third type of structured group activity. This scenario has obviously no relationship to the likely experience of any of us, except perhaps astronauts, and the likelihood of similar circumstances arising with them is also highly unlikely. Although the actual situation in which the problem-solving group finds itself is unreal, the very real lessons which can be drawn from its process include:

- analysis
- planning
- problem-solving
- decision-making
- team building
- group behaviour
- individual behaviour
- identification of value judgements and life attitudes
- assertiveness
- communication.

Planning and design

The primary reason for using an activity is that it has a relationship with satisfying the objectives of the particular or general learning programme, it is not just an amusing interlude. An activity rarely stands alone as the vehicle for producing the learning, rather it acts as a strong support for the more formal approach to the learning – an input session, video, computer program and so on – and is used in conjunction with these. I have mentioned the length of time necessary for activities – this is certainly true of structured group activities, and so considerable planning of their inclusion must take place before the programme. Consequently the overall objective for an activity must be that its objectives must correlate completely with those of the learning pro-gramme and support any other related form of learning within the programme.

The reasons for activities can include:

- discussion of the topic that is to be or has been discussed;
- the solution of a problem, normally using the techniques deter-mined in preceding learning events;
- performing a skills task as practice of techniques determined in preceding learning events;
- performing a skills task to assess the skill level of the learners at particular stages of the learning event.

In the last case, this activity might be at the start of an event to assess the learners' starting levels, during the event to assess their develop-ment, or at the end as a final assessment of their learning of the programme objectives.

It is often suggested that every knowledge input should be supple-mented by an activity to ensure that the learning is actually achieved – this achievement being demonstrated by the successful performance of the activity. This is true in the majority of cases, but there can be a danger of training/trainer rejection by the learning group if, eg a simple learn-ing lesson is followed by an activity which is obviously designed to give practice in the factor – when equally obviously this inclusion is both unnecessary and patronizing.

Timing

There are two aspects of timing: the time taken by the activity itself, and the placement of the activity in a particular part of the programme. Notice will have been taken of the latter in the planning stage when the decision is made to include an activity and what form this activity will take. The possible location at the start of, during and at the end of an event or part of an event has already been discussed – this location is a major relevance in the timing of the activity. But it raises a serious question that is also linked to the other aspect. Apart from the simple introductions, icebreakers and energizers, most significant activities require a substantial amount of time for their performance. 'Perform-ance' obviously includes planning, preparation, briefing, doing and reviewing. Few structured group activities that have worthwhile results can be performed in much less than 45 minutes (briefing, activity and review) and the majority can take much longer. Typically, the briefing part (if observers are not to have substantial preparation) can take something of the order of ten minutes, the activity part of the event has a minimum timing of 20 minutes and the review period, which depends of course on the method used and the number of subgroups, at least 30 minutes. (One aspect that is often forgotten in planning the time to be allotted is the time that the groups take to go to their syndicate rooms and return to the main room at the end of the activity.) A straightforward approach such as this quickly adds up to 70 minutes or so, a substantial part of a training day.

This, of course, has a bearing on the decision of most trainers – although they would like to make their learning events experiential they simply cannot afford the time involved. Not that the time used is wasted, but their organizations have given them a restricted period in which to achieve specific objectives, and in order to complete these trainers are forced to offer training in a form that is less than satisfactory. It is simple for pundits to disclaim such restrictions, advocating that the trainers have the constraints varied or that the learning can be achieved in the allotted time, but practising trainers know that such ideals and ideologies are difficult to attain in real life.

Life is usually a compromise! If you are plagued by the problems outlined above your options are to:

- omit activities (the last resort);
- choose ones that take a restricted time to perform;
- reduce the review period (again a 'last resort' action, although at times the review process can be varied).

Grouping

The various methods of forming groups for activities has been considered earlier, but it is worth remembering that this may not be a simple affair with little significance. Typical comments by learners after a series of activities can include:

- 'Why did I have to change groups? I was getting along so well with that group.'
- 'Why did we have to stay in the same group all the time? I didn't like the other members and I wanted to work with other people.'
- 'I would have liked to have stayed with the group which contained people from my organization so we could relate the situations to our culture.'
- 'I would have liked to have been in different groups with people from other organizations. I'm sure they have different approaches to the ones we have.'

Notice how the examples of comments, all of which I have heard, are contradictory one with the other; they can happen on virtually any learning programme with any group of people. I am not suggesting that the views and feelings of the learners should be ignored, in fact the wise trainer checks out these attitudes as the event progresses, but the objectives of the programme must also be taken into account.

It may be that a group of high contributors/reactors are not learning through being included in one subgroup in spite of their behaviour being reviewed. Consequently, because the event objectives are concerned with behaviour, the trainer might decide to repeat and open up the learning opportunity by having the same group of people together again (and again?).

If the learning involves reinforcing a new technique that has different applications in different organizations that are represented on the event, it makes sense to group familiars and if necessary maintain that grouping.

Structured group activities can suggest the whole spectrum of learner groupings, again with the decision dominated by the needs of the programme linked with those of the learning group. If a number of opportunities to practise similar techniques, or progressive parts of such techniques, is provided, care must be taken to ensure that as many learners as possible can take the major learning roles. This can be achieved mainly by a predetermined rota system.

Other groupings, depending on the learning event needs, can be random. In such cases I have used the 'even numbers round the group for one group' approach; for the next activity, 'odd numbers round the group'; for the next one alternately seated members, and so on. Not scientific, but it has the advantage of simplicity, as long as you remember which system you used previously.

Where the population of subgroups has no major influence on the event, a most satisfactory approach is to give the learners the responsibility for:

- choosing their first groups;
- deciding whether to maintain these groups after one or two activities;
- with guidance and advice, deciding which grouping will serve their needs the most.

The question of groupings and their maintenance, if the learning ideal of heterogeneous mixing is not the most significant factor and the personal wishes of the participants would negate the learning opportunities, must take these and other factors into account in the first instance.

Resources

Every activity has a number of resource demands:

- briefs for the participants;
- briefs for the observers;
- rooms for the subgroups, or their own private space in a single large room;
- relevant materials;
- support material – paper, pens, flipcharts, markers and so on. One aspect on which I have found many trainers fall down is the provision of flipchart paper and markers. It is so easy for the learners to use more paper than was estimated and they almost invariably bring the markers back to the main room and forget to return them!

Each activity will possibly require different resources, so it is very helpful to have a file for each activity you are going to include in the learning event. Keep these in order of use and in each folder include:

- the required number of briefs for the number of learners (plus one or two as contingency copies);
- the required number of activity briefs and observer briefs for the number of observers; plus
- a checklist of the method of running the activity including a clear statement of any instructions to be given verbally;
- a checklist of resources required, as described above;
- a checklist of the essential learning points that must be brought out in the review, whichever method is used.

Methods

Every activity will obviously have its own procedure and instructions and, as suggested above, an activity folder can include a prepared sheet detailing these. But there is a general approach to running structured group activities which overlays any specific instructions or procedures. This can be summarized as:

1. Introduce the activity in brief, simple terms that explain the reason (but not necessarily the final result). Also describe the method by which the activity will be reviewed.
2. Allocate subgroup rooms and give directions for finding them.
3. Issue the briefs to the activity participants and allocate a specific timed period for familiarization (remember, however, that some

activities require this familiarization/interpretation to be part of the activity itself).

4. Issue copies of the activity briefs given to the participants to the observers in addition to their own observation briefs. These can be studied and discussed while the participants are studying their own briefs. If the participants are not given pre-activity time, they might be asked to review the learning material relevant to the activity while the observers are considering.

5. Seek clarification questions about the process of the activity, but not about the way the task itself should be performed.

6. Ask the subgroups to go to their rooms, and define the time they have to complete the activity – stating the finishing time rather than a vague '20 minutes or so.'

7. A few minutes after the subgroups have dispersed visit the rooms, not to intervene, but to check that they have everything they require, if they have any process (not task) questions and to stay for one or two minutes to observe progress. Do this with all groups.

8. Take action on your predetermined role, whether this is complete withdrawal, intermittent visiting of all groups, or staying with one group. This last action should only be taken if there are other trainers who can do the same with the other groups.

9. Visit the groups a few minutes before the due finishing time to warn them of the approaching end of the event and to remind them of any reporting requirements.

10. Ensure that the subgroups finish at the due time and have the reporting requirements with them to bring to the main room.

11. Take the agreed review action as described earlier – this may involve immediate review, review following completion of activity *aide-mémoires* or return to the subgroups to have a debriefing with the subgroup observers.

12. If necessary, have a short, final, significant learning full group review to end the activity in a positive and summarizing atmosphere.

13. Either have a review conversation with yourself or with any other trainers involved to discuss the success of the activity and to identify any other follow-up action necessary.

Role playing

The problem of artificiality is frequently raised after activities, particularly where (as often happens), the learners are asked to take on roles, sometimes close to their own personalities or jobs, sometimes completely opposite to these and sometimes completely artificial. It is simpler if in an activity the participants can behave as they would normally, in spite of the artificiality of the situation, but this is not always possible or even desirable. The roles they are asked to play, apart from extreme cases, are usually real roles but included specially for that activity. Acting requirements should be kept to a minimum although some may be necessary – when considering the inclusion of an activity you should always consider the extent to which this would be required; I have turned down some activities because they would require too extreme a form of acting. Most people can, however, act a rather different role to their norm. After all, we are changing roles all the time – at work, at home, as partner, parent, football match spectator, socializer and so on. But it is almost a certainty that you will get the excuse from participants for their 'failure' that they couldn't act the role.

Most trainers think of roles in one-to-one activities, where one participant is taking on the (unusual for them) role of the manager or supervisor and the other participant that of the problem-owner. But roles can also be required in structured group activities, the most common being in skill-type developmental events. A typical one is that of negotiating skills when during activities each learner has to take on a role of, say, a salesperson, an organization lead negotiator, a hard negotiator, a soft negotiator and so on. Or, a favourite one for meetings training, is where a committee meets with different personae – the trade union representative, the employers' representative, the local councillor, the local government official, the national government officer, the social worker and of course the chairperson. Most of the learners involved will find these roles strange to them as practitioners, although they will almost certainly have encountered them at some time, so they will not be completely alien. This latter familiarity is something to aim for in activities to help the process.

Resources

The number of structured group activities used by trainers and/or published in collection runs into hundreds, probably more than one thousand. This in itself presents problems for the trainer who wants to select a different activity for his or her programme. Many collections cover all types of situation, although those more recently published have tended to concentrate on specific groups of activity types. This narrows the search somewhat, but it can still present a difficult problem. Many trainers have favourite activities, and fortunately many activities can be modified to suit a variety of situations. If the range of activities is examined carefully it will be seen that many are in fact variations of a basic theme, some cleverly contrived to be different, some almost word for word copies, others exact copies but with the names and places altered.

'Artificial' activities tend to become the favourites of trainers, particularly because they can be manipulated to ensure that the essential learning points are included and can emerge in the activity. These activities can cover the full range of skills that are included in training programmes.

THE HUMAN ZOO

Ken Jones is a prolific producer of interesting and usable activities, and one of my favourites published by him is entitled 'The Human Zoo' (Jones, 1993). This activity gives a group of people the brief that a message has been received from a group of aliens that have arrived in the vicinity of Earth. This message is an ultimatum for a decision on the setting up for the aliens of a human zoo on Earth. The participants, who are given roles as representatives of the various areas of Earth, each with their own selfish needs and demands, have the task of making a decision about the problem, or having the Earth eliminated. The activity requires a minimum of five participants – if there are more in the learning group, observers can be appointed, and/or other roles can be added, or two subgroups can be formed to perform the activity in parallel.

The activity can be used with a variety of objectives, including:

- meeting leadership procedures;
- meeting leadership behaviours;
- meeting member behaviours;
- planning;
- problem-solving;
- decision-making;
- the resolution of differing viewpoints;
- the enhancement of diplomacy;
- the use and abuse of 'hidden agendas';
- the resolution of race differences and problems.

The activity with five participants can last about an hour, longer with more participants as more people will want to have a say and there may be more conflict to be resolved.

THE MAST EXERCISE

This is another of my favourites whose roots are lost in the past and which can be used with a variety of objectives in mind. Many people have had experience of this activity or its numerous derivatives, but I am still surprised by the number who haven't, and who really enjoy the experience. I have not carried out any real research on this, but I have the feeling that it is enjoyed more by men than women, not only because of the competitiveness generated, but also because most men are really little boys at heart!

The activity, which involves building a mast with Lego bricks, at maximum profit, is divided into two parts, and I have found that it works most effectively with two or more subgroups of four participants, each group with an observer. The first part, for which 20 minutes is allocated, no initial briefing being given, is the planning period. During this the learners can use the bricks to practise building masts, using graphs of brick, height and time costs supplied to them. This period is observed by the observer who is particularly looking at:

- the way in which the leader explains the task;
- the use that is made of the graphs;
- how these are analyzed and used;
- the existing experience in the group of graph analysis and the use of Lego bricks;
- the use of all the participants;
- the behaviour of the participants with each other.

At the end of this planning period the groups declare their intentions and profit aims, and in the time that they decide (usually between five and ten minutes), in sight of each other, they build their mast, which is then measured and brick use counted.

As you will imagine the review session can be quite active and extended, with competitive attitudes emerging quickly along with the laying of blame. The objectives for an activity of this nature are almost endless and can cover almost every aspect of a manager's skill requirements. It is rarely accused of being childish, particularly after the extensive review session, and I have used it effectively with groups ranging over clerical and secretarial workers through supervisors, managers and directors.

THE NEGOTIATED DEAL

This activity, which can be artificial, work or personal/social based, has almost innumerable variants. In its basic form it is a paired negotiation over some aspect, and used in a learning group has a number of pairs negotiating at the same time, one of each pair identifiable as the 'lead' negotiator, the other as the 'proposing' negotiator. The 'lead' negotiators are part of a team, as are the 'proposers', and prior to the paired events each team meets to agree its objectives, positions and all the other learning aspects of negotiating. An observer can be used with each pair, but I have found that feedback comes very easily from the parties involved.

The principal objectives of an activity of this nature are obviously for the learners to practise what they have learned and for the trainers to assess the progress of the learners. The approach described above also suggests elements of team work and competitiveness, behavioural attitudes, planning, preparation, communication, assertiveness and so on, as in the case of so many structured group activities.

Used carefully and with effective planning and preparation, the inclusion of structured group activities in learning events can encourage, simplify and enhance learning and the transfer of the learning to the practicalities of work.

References

Jones, Ken (1993) *Imaginative Events, Volume 1*, The McGraw-Hill Training Series (one of two volumes of innovative simulations, exercises, puzzles and games).

10

—

Case Studies and Simulations

These are all extensions of structured activities with specific applications in training and development, all requiring more complex and extended setting up than the previously described activities.

CASE STUDIES

Case studies are activities that provide examples of a task subject for the learners to consider, discuss and perform. They are very relevant to the subject under discussion in the programme, whether this is a specific part of the programme or the programme as a whole. However, probably the most obvious difference between a case study and many other structured group activities is that the latter are usually process based, the actual task being less important than how it is performed, whereas case studies are firmly content or task based.

A complete historical record of the background of the organization included in the study is provided, often including material that is not necessary for the performance of the task, but always including the data from which the task might be completed. This data can be completely imaginary or, preferably, based on a real organizational situation. The closer to the real event, the more acceptable will be the study, with errors and omissions less likely.

From the historical data the learners are presented with a problem to be solved, additional, newer data being made available as necessary. The learning groups make recommendations for the solution of the problem, acceptance of which can be by either the trainer or an invited line manager from the linked organization as relevant. I have found the latter approach the more satisfactory as the learners will afford the practising line manager more credibility in this instance that the trainers, however generally acceptable and credible they might be.

Membership

In most case study activities the whole group is included on a participant basis in order to give everybody the opportunity to be involved in the activity, with the trainer frequently acting as observer. Observers can be used from the learning group, but the situation must be watched carefully as case studies tend to continue longer than the previously described structured activities. In any case, the trainer must be available during the study activity to provide any further information required.

Timing

This is a very variable item as the length of time necessary for the learners to complete the case study will depend on its complexity. However, a substantial period of time will be essential, as not only do the learners have to go through the process of problem-solving and decision-making but, before they can move to these stages, the wealth of information has to be read, discussed and analyzed. Time can be saved by requiring the learners to read the material as individuals before they attend the programme. It is essential that when this material is sent prior to the programme the importance of coming to the programme with a good understanding of the case is understood and acted on. Consequently, the learner group's preparation period can be considerably reduced by ensuring that everybody has read and understood the information provided.

Planning and design

The planning requirements for a case study include:

- the decision on whether to use an artificial or a real problem;
- how far the study will extend – a complete organizational problem, specific managerial problems or personal value situations;
- the resources to be made available – a written brief, a video clip (commercially or 'home'-produced) or a computer application;
- whether observers will be used, how and to what extent;
- the role to be taken by the trainer(s) during the activity;
- the format of the review.

You will find the task of constructing an artificial case study easier if it is based on actual organizational situations, which will also make the study more acceptable to the learners. Whether the case study is artificial or real, the historical data should be complete and honest, ie without any 'deliberate mistakes' to cause the learners even more problems. This is one training situation where line management can be successfully involved in the planning process, particularly if you can find a manager who has experienced the types of problems you want to include in the study.

Reports, organization charts, job descriptions and so on may all be needed in considerable quantities, and may need modification to make them more suitable for training purposes. Trainers who use real case studies usually find that they spend a lot of time in producing the initial study which can then, with only amendments or updates, last for a long time. Of course, not all case studies need to be as fully extensive as the type described, but even a relatively small study must contain a lot of background detail if the learners are to be successful.

If the material and the required activity are particularly extensive and complex, the study activity can be broken down into stages, perhaps ones that might relate to the progress of the learning programme. For example, one stage might be concerned with the collection and analysis of data, another with problem-solving and solution generation and yet another with decision-making and implementation.

Your preparation time will almost certainly be longer than in the case of the structured activity. The objectives and 'answers' to the short, structured activity are usually relatively simple and require a minimum of review by you prior to the activity. However, with case studies, because of their complexity, the objectives and possible results can be equally complex. You will need to be absolutely clear about the objectives of the study and to have considered all the possible options that could be suggested, the ones that would be more favourable and the reasons for these choices. This consideration should not be so that you can disagree with the results produced by the learners, but you may have to suggest that they reconsider or consider other options.

In this respect it is useful to construct a checklist showing:

1. the process points that you or an observer should be looking for while the group is performing the study;
2. the range of possible recommendations with summarized comments against each.

Your selection of the subgroups (if these are used) will possibly need to be more selective than in the case of general structured group activities. Because there may be financial, operational, production, administrative information and problems in the study, if at all possible each group should include a learner who is knowledgeable (or more knowledgeable that the remainder) in these topics. Otherwise, a balanced selection according to attitudes and observed behaviour might be the way you would proceed.

Usage

The method of use of a case study is basically the same as with the structured group activity, the principal difference being that of scale. This process will be:

- Depending on the complexity of the study and the number of learners available or needed for a successful approach to the study, divide the learning group into subgroups. It is recommended that the optimum number of learners in a subgroup will be about six for a complex case study.
- If the case study itself has been sent to the learners prior to the programme, give the sub-groups time to reread the information, discuss it among themselves and clarify as far as possible any non- or misunderstandings. The trainer should be available to clarify any points of information that cannot be cleared by the group.
- Issue the activity brief and again be available to clarify as necessary.
- The activity progresses, with or without observers or the presence of the trainer.
- After the activity the process and task are reviewed in the manner agreed – in plenary or with observer feedback followed by plenary.

The activity brief, as suggested earlier, can range from a relatively simple task requirement from the information to resolving a complex and complicated problem.

The simpler cases will be similar to structured activities and can include, eg a management skill of dealing with people problems. The background is described fully and the group will be required to consider all the factors involved and suggest options for dealing with the problem in a practical way.

More complex cases, in addition to the historical data provided, may produce an extension of the case study in the form of additional or changed information, with the requirement being placed on the learners to produce recommendations for the solution of the problem.

A more complex case study

At the issue of the brief stage in the process of the activity, the instructions could be:

'Attached to this general brief are company reports, financial and audit reports, operational reports and statements by the managers concerned, which show that there is a problem in the company in operation production. This problem started a year ago and has increased in size during that period.

From the historical data given to you and also this new information:

- identify the problem and its extent;
- identify the location of the problem;
- produce optional approaches to solving the problem;
- recommend from these options the most favoured one, taking into account cost, time, resources and the requirement by the Board that the problem disappears within six months of implementation of the solution;
- recommend how the solution implementation can be monitored and its success evaluated;
- summarize your actions and recommendations on flipchart sheets and be prepared to present these to the other group and the trainer [a line manager], including any minority dissension reports.'

This is obviously a complex case study, although less complex ones might have similar briefs. The objective set for such a case study would include the requirements that the learners:

- understand the historical data about the organization and its implications, and describe the organization in these terms;
- are able to systematically collect and analyze data;
- are able to analyze additional information;
- are able to identify correctly the problem(s) produced by the new information, ignoring or discounting spurious problems;
- are able to work together as a problem-solving group in the most effective manner possible and effectively communicate with each other;
- produce in a systematic manner a range of possible solutions and identify the optimum solution(s) from this list;
- recommend the most favourable solution (which should be one of those in the 'expert's' selected solutions);
- are able to present and argue their actions and findings before any other subgroups, the trainer(s) and/or the line manager/expert.

Reviewing

The basic approach to reviewing the case study activity can include any of the methods described in Chapter 6, but in this case the concentration will be on both the content or task bases of the activity and the processes involved. Because the learning group has been so immersed in solving an actual, practical problem, the review will be best initiated with an analysis of their task results, rather than the more qualitative aspects of the process. The checklist recommended earlier will help in this review, which in most instances of case studies will be led by the trainer and/or line manager/expert.

The type of task review questions will include:

- What was the problem identified? Were there any other problems? What were they and what did the group do or consider doing about them?
- What was the range of possible solutions produced?
- Which possible solutions were considered to be the optimum ones and why?
- What did the group decide about how the most favoured solution might be implemented, monitored and assessed?

(At the relevant stages, the group(s) can be asked to refer to and present the information they have entered on their flipchart sheets.)

The checklist will also give guidelines on the types of process questions to ask and these will include:

- How accurate was their analysis of the information?
- How accurate was their diagnosis of the situation following the receipt of the additional/new information and statement that a problem existed?
- Did they consider all relevant important information, or did they miss any significant aspects? What happened as a result of the latter and how was it rectified?
- How difficult did they find the task? Which aspects of the task did they find more difficult than others and why?
- What problems did they encounter when approaching the problem-solving, solution-generating section of the task? What were these and how did they deal with them?
- What problems did they encounter in recommending the optimum solution(s)?

You will see from the foregoing that if both content and process are reviewed a lot of information is required, resulting in a considerable amount of discussion, particularly if more than one subgroup worked on the study with differing results. This will take some time, but the case study would obviously not be included if insufficient time could not be allowed for a full review. A number of developmental programmes use case studies of the complex nature and the full programme is in fact built around the case study. In such cases, time will be adjusted according to what is available and the number of stages involved.

One aid to the learners for the review period would be to reproduce a checklist of the main questions – content and process – similar to the one you will be using. Immediately following the end of the study activity, but before the review, give a copy to each participant and give them some time to reflect on what happened in the activity in terms of the checklist items.

Problems

One other problem, which in fact can also occur with the shorter structured group activities, can be that the task will actually get in the way of the learning. The learners can become so involved and interested in the task problem that they find it difficult to relate what they have done to any learning aspects. The completion of the task becomes the only feature in their minds. You should remind the participants at the start of the activity that it is a learning activity in which they might become over involved, but that they should try to notice events happening as the activity proceeds – a lot to ask! Otherwise, they should be encouraged to consider the process incidents during their post-activity reflection period – usually if they think back to the activity, a number will remember incidents which can often be built into a fairly comprehensive picture of the process.

Using case studies is not easy – for either you or the learners – but most experience shows that learners enjoy these activities because of their closeness to real life and the real challenges they offer. Successful completion is very satisfying for all concerned – as well as offering the opportunity to involve line managers in training and development.

THE IN-TRAY OR IN-BASKET ACTIVITY

Description

This is a form of case study that will be familiar to many learners who have attended training and development programmes. It is a simpler alternative to the complex case studies described above. It simulates a 'typical' office in-tray (sometimes referred to as an in-basket) with a wide variety of contents – reports, memoranda, notes, requests for information, requests for interviews, invitations, letters and so on. The purpose of the activity is to have the learners sort these items according to learned criteria and, where necessary, take action.

The in-tray contents are effectively related to the subjects included in the learning programme in which the activity is contained. For example, if the programme is concerned with negotiation skills training, most of the in-tray contents will have a negotiation bias.

Membership

The activity can be performed with or without observers, most frequently without as it is basically an individual exercise which can be assessed to a large extent by the results. The options, however, can include operation either on an individual basis, or with individuals grouped into subgroups or teams, or as a group exercise.

Timing

As with most activities this will vary with the number of learners involved and the complexity of the activity, but this activity will be planned to last the minimum time possible. The restriction of time places stress on the participants, another relationship to the real world of work in which the usually slower pace of a training programme is not always reflected. The time allotted must, however, be reasonable and, with a newly created activity, will need to be determined through trial and error.

Planning and design

The activity is centred around a number of documents related to the objectives of the exercise. These objectives will need to be clear from the start, although usually this type of activity has fairly specific, albeit general objectives. These objectives include:

- the systematic and speedy reading and understanding of a variety of written communications;
- effective analysis of the documents inspected;
- identification of the documents in terms of:
  - urgency;
  - importance;
  - urgent but not important;
  - important but not urgent;
  - neither urgent nor important;
- deciding from the classification which items need to be dealt with and how this should be done;
- taking decided action in the most appropriate way – writing a memo, making a phone call, making a personal visit and so on;
- keeping effective records of action taken.

In order to satisfy these objectives, the collection of documents placed in the in-tray, other than for specific learning situations, should include:

- complex reports for the next Board meeting (say in three weeks time);
- conflicting time or resource demands;
- decisions required – urgent etc;
- invitations – to meetings, social functions, talks, association meetings;
- letters – internal, external;
- queries;
- requests for information – simple, complex;
- simple internal memos – from boss, from staff, from peers.

In some of the documents that require or request contact with other people, their imminent absence or non-availability should be mentioned which might coincide with your own absence.

Usage

The principal objective of the in-tray activity is to have the participants, using the in-tray contents in the manner described above, come to decisions about the documents and take action. In order to accurately reflect the real-life situation and also to introduce a significant element of stress and urgency, a further factor is introduced. This is that the in-tray decisions etc must be made in a specific period of time because you:

- as manager and owner of the in-tray, are leaving to attend a week-long meeting in another city;
- are going on holiday for two weeks in a remote area where you will not be accessible;
- are going into hospital for an operation, will be there for two weeks, including convalescence, during which you must not be contacted;

and similar situations that restrict the time available for the in-tray to be cleared.

The procedure for using an in-tray activity might therefore be along the following lines:

- Introduce the activity in general terms, describing briefly the objectives and methods – individuals, individuals in teams, groups.
- Divide the learning group into groups of individuals or groups as necessary.
- Issue each participant or group (in the third method) with a set of the in-tray contents.
- Brief observers if they are being used.
- State the time at which the activity will terminate.
- Commence the activity:
  (a) individuals completing their own in-tray;
  (b) individuals completing their own in-tray, followed by a meeting of the group to discuss, argue and decide on a final group decision;
  (c) the groups completing, as a group, the in-tray decisions;
- Review the activity as discussed in Chapter 6.

The review (which, because observers are not normally used in this type of activity, will be led by the trainer) can usefully include questions covering:

- what decisions they made;
- why they made those particular decisions;
- what alternative choices there might be – at this stage individuals or groups can be given the opportunity to question others on why they chose one path rather than another (usually their path!) and to discuss the benefits of varying decisions;
- the procedures used in approaching the activity;
- how they think the recipients of the messages will feel;
- any problem items that gave them particular difficulty or they were unable to deal with;
- how they went about the activity;
- what their views were on the time allocation.

SIMULATION

Description

Simulations have many similarities to case studies (from which they stem), but are much more extensive, usually more complex and require the learners to take on individual roles, rather than only be part of a group, albeit a role-playing member of that group. They are working representations of reality, being an attempt to model a complex process in the safer atmosphere of a training and development programme. In simulations the learners take on 'real' roles, more real in some simulations than others. Every attempt is made to produce a simulation as near to real-life working as possible, and in many cases, although still in a training and development environment, this is achieved through the reality of the simulation. But because of the training and development situation you must ensure that no harm comes to the participants, as could occur in real life. In most cases this will be 100 per cent effective, but when the simulation involves people having to interact with others there will always be the possibility of unfortunate or negative interactions.

Simulations can be people interacting with 'things' – devices, computers, models – or with other people in a full or part organizational context. The situations that are simulated as models can range over the abstract, the simple, the accelerated or slowed-down, the many populated or people limited. A simulation is a highly active (usually highly interactive) process that allows people to discuss, analyze, reflect on, propose action, act, review, amend and cover almost every role or organizational process in a manner certainly not possible in the real world at work, nor as extensively in other forms of training.

Membership

In all simulations, in one way or another, every participant becomes involved and has a specific role to play. For example, in simulations that model the particular requirements of an organization all the learners are involved at the same time, each with active roles. In other simulations, eg in a trainer development programme where the simulation might be concerned with trainers in co-working, one section of the group will have one set of roles (presenters), another a different set (audience) and yet another a third set (appraisers). Rarely, except in cases like the second example, do the learners act as observers and even then, although the observation and appraisal is real, they are taking roles – those of practitioner trainers. Usually, because all members are actively involved, the trainer, or in many cases a team of trainers will be the observers, although at the end of the simulation much of the review will be performed by the learners themselves.

Timing

The timing of simulations within a training programme and the length of time allotted and utilized will obviously again depend on the complexity of the simulation and its type. The full organizational simulation can extend over several days, according to the size, complexity and problems of the organization and the problem set for the learners. Such an extended simulation can, in fact, be the learning programme, the simulation having been designed so that all the desired objectives form part of the simulation, with the review following it consolidating this learning through doing. Or a similar type of simulation can be preceded by some input and lesser activities using the skills that the learners would need to perform the simulation successfully.

If the simulation is only part of the full job role it will require less active time and can occur at any time during the programme, being preceded and followed perhaps by other aspects of the roles or model.

In any case, whatever the form and complexity of the simulation, a significant block of time will be necessary for the learners–trainers to plan, design, prepare, produce and review the simulation and for the learners to take as active and full a part as possible.

Planning and design

A simulation is a powerful learning medium, and as such requires a considerable amount of preparation of materials and environment and of trainer energy, the actual extent depending on the size and complexity of the simulation. These preparatory demands, as well as the unpredictability of the process and result, the stress on the learners and the potential scale of failure, are probably the reasons why simulations are underused in general forms of training.

Most types of organization simulation will require extensive research by the trainer to be able to provide full case material – reports, financial statements, accounting reports, operational and production reports and charts, personnel and staff reports, statistics of a variety of aspects, and so on – what amounts to a detailed data base of the organization. As with case studies, a simulation is an ideal opportunity for the training department to involve line management in the learning programme. These line managers are not only the people who possess the base material, but also have had practical experience of the situations modelled in the simulation, and may have been involved in the problems raised. Again, as in case studies, these line managers/experts can be involved in the process of the simulation as resources, contingency clarifiers, but with a firm brief not to solve the problem for the learners. They can also be invaluable in the review process part of the simulation.

The administration requirements for setting up a simulation, particularly a new one, are formidable, and can involve the arrangements for all or some of the following:

- all paper resources – reports etc;
- the simulation briefs for the learners;
- a number of rooms;
- computers;
- video recorders and playback equipment;
- working materials and stationery – telephones, faxes and other office or situation equipment;
- expert availability;
- trainer team availability and development.

The papers will contain as much information about the organization as necessary for the learners to solve the problems posed, information only being held back if this would be the case in the real world, the learners needing to request it. The brief must also contain as much clear information as is necessary to set the learners off on the problem they have to solve or the identifications they have to make. This is a substantial amount of material, with a copy being made available for each participant. Time must be allowed for them to study the papers and assimilate the information they need to start the simulation.

In an organizational simulation a number of rooms modelling some of the rooms of the actual organization, though on a reduced scale, will probably be necessary. Separate rooms might be needed for different role groups – directors, production managers, sales managers, finance and accounts and so on. The scale of a simulation of this nature will accordingly have more needs than is usual in most training programmes.

A few years ago the process of a simulation was an unwieldy matter, with all the activities being enacted manually. But now the availability of computer technology such as multi-media can simplify or at least speed up the activities. Financial reports and statistics can be presented on spreadsheets on the computer rather than on sheets of paper, and the participants can manipulate the entries as the simulation progresses. A mass of information can be stored on the computer and, in addition to providing manipulative data for the participants, it can be readily amended and updated as necessary by the trainer as the organization changes with time. The simulation may even involve the use of a computer network between the parts of the modelled organization.

There are many arguments – unresolved – about the use of video recording in a simulation. Certainly the video medium is an excellent vehicle for providing information, data, descriptions and so on – either instead of or in support of written, verbal or computer material. But the doubts that you need to resolve for your simulation are concerned with the invasiveness of the video camera during a simulation in which an attempt is being made to replicate the real world, the placing and operation of the equipment, the use of recordings for the review and the overall value as opposed to 'manual' observation and feedback. The invasiveness will be a reducing factor with time as the participants become accustomed to the video camera's presence. But in an extensive simulation a lot of videoing would result in constraints on the roles of the trainers. In many ways the use of video resolves many problems and produces much data, but you have to weigh this against all the operational problems described.

Usage

Simulations have a wide range of usage, in many cases the only restriction being the scale of a simulation, rather than a simpler case study or structured group activity. Some of these uses can be in:

- Trainer development programmes – as described earlier, the practice of co-working can be modelled, as can presentations in general or any of the activities in which a trainer might have to engage. One trainer development programme in which I was involved for several years gave the learner–trainers the opportunity to learn many of the skills and techniques of the trainer and practise these to a limited extent in role plays, case studies and structured group activities. The training programme culminated with a simulation of a short training course for which the learners had to plan, produce objectives, decide and design sessions and activities, produce briefs and observational instruments, construct review methods and any instruments necessary, arrange for video equipment and so on – all the aspects in which a practitioner–trainer would be involved in setting up an actual training event. In this case the practitioner–trainers were a major source of information and resource, but the range of other resources available to the learners was extensive. The process was for the learners, in two separate groups, to perform this short training programme using the other group as the 'trainees'.

- Management development – this is an area in which simulations have an extensive potential for use, and the situations modelled can be, as described above, the identification and solution of problems besetting an organization, or part of an organization; the setting up of an organization or section, or perhaps relocation; solving 'what if' types of problems; designing and introducing new procedures; practising management skills and so on.

- Skill practice, licence renewal – the best-known and well-used example of this is the flight simulator for aircraft pilots. When new pilots are under training, experienced pilots need to be assessed, operational or equipment changes are introduced, or general training is required, the pilots and other crew members enter a flight simulator. This computer-based, aircraft cockpit mock-up can be made to simulate every flight situation conceivable, including some that a pilot would hope never to have to experience. Take-offs, landing, crises during flight and emergency operations can all be simulated almost as if the pilot and crew were actually in a real aircraft. Obviously, all these activities can take place in absolute safety, and with the availability of review and assessment.

- General problem-solving – the problem-solving possibilities are not restricted to industrial and commercial organizations, and the extension to other areas is very similar in format. For example, a learning group might be trainee town and country planners and the simulation would be in the development of an area linked to this. They might be given a set of data which describes the terrain and geography of a part of a country or small country, the natural resources present, the climatic conditions, existing population areas, existing and/or proposed industries and commercial organizations, sea resources and so on. They might be asked to identify the economic or ecological problems that exist and how they might be approached, or they might be asked to produce an economic development policy and/or strategy for the next decade. In addition to the factual information, local and national government proposals are issued and media reports and issues are raised. The range of such simulations is almost endless.

It may be that simulations of this nature are too complex to be part of training programmes, but the world of computer 'games' has exploded this myth to a certain extent. Currently available are simulation games that replicate the simulations so far described, simulations that even children can take part in. The bases of these simulations, for example 'SimCity 2000', 'SimTower', 'Transport Tycoon' and so on, are that the operator is in almost complete charge of the activity, uses money in a virtual reality, works in competition with other operators (live companions or computer generated), can add or delete (at costs) aspects related to the game, etc. For example, in 'Transport Tycoon' the PC operator can design a world with topographical details in the terrain; create industries and banks; build and operate road, rail, air and sea networks etc. Each action costs money from an original amount, and the services can bring in money, the principal objectives being to make as much money as possible in the time allowed and beat the competitors. The rules and procedures can be complex, but certainly nine- or ten-year-olds can perform the simulations very successfully and in so doing learn a lot about the operation of the real world.

Methods

The methods of introducing, enacting and closing a simulation are little different from those of other training activities and can be summarized as:

1. Introduce the simulation and describe its relationship to reality.
2. Select or agree learner selection of roles.
3. Issue simulation data information, whether printed and/or computer/video based, and allow sufficient time for the learners to assimilate the information.
4. Issue the simulation brief which will include the simulation objectives.
5. Allow the simulation to run, with limited or no trainer intervention (as suggested earlier, line managers/experts can be used during this stage).
6. At the end of the simulation, because even more than in other training activities the learners may have completely related to the activity, allow time for the learners to 'come back to earth'. The learners can be helped in this by a substantial break, or a period of reflection and reflective instrument completion.
7. Hold an extensive review which will consider:
   - whether the objectives were achieved;
   - how they were achieved. What/who helped or hindered the process?
   - what the individual role feelings, actions, reactions were;
   - how the role players felt about their fellow role players? What

actions produced what reactions and feelings?
- what changes occurred over the simulation – and why;
- what conclusions were reached at the end;
- what learning the learners felt they achieved from the simulation.

Because of the complex and extensive nature of this event, it is usual for the trainer team to lead the review, but a number of variations are possible (some are even desirable). The role groups can be reviewed as a group with a trainer accompanying each group, then a plenary session held to bring out the universal significances. It is difficult for the learners to take control of the review in the full group, but this becomes much more possible in the division into role groups. Whichever approach is used, the involvement of the learners – their views, feelings, experiences, attitudes – must be introduced to the maximum extent. After all, these learners will have expended a lot of time, energy and emotion in the simulation – it was their simulation – and consequently need to claim and comment on this ownership.

Summary

Some significant aspects of simulations can be summarized as:

- Simulations are usually problem-solving activities modelled on real situations and are set in motion by a requirement on the learners to identify and solve any problems.
- Solutions are flexible, not singular and not 'cut and dried'.
- Participants perform roles which may or may not reflect their own job roles.
- Roles can be selected by the trainer from knowledge of the learners' jobs or to simulate other behaviours and roles, or self-selected by the learners.
- The simulation cannot be predicted accurately, as much of the progress will be dependent on the learners themselves.
- Participants develop a 'reality' or special relationship with their roles and consequently strong emotions and feelings can be generated during (and after!) the simulation.
- Simulations can range from the simple to the highly complex, world models, and can be people and organization based or directly related to a skill with resources.
- Simulations are probably the most complex and difficult training activity to prepare and perform, but a successful simulation can produce learning rewards unobtainable by any other approach.

11

One-to-One Interactions

Description

The description of one-to-one interactions or activities used in this book is where two people take part in a learning activity in which they interact with each other for the purpose of learning. They do this by taking on roles – manager, subordinate, supplicant, disciplinarian, person being disciplined and so on. The term 'role play' is frequently applied loosely to describe these activities, but I prefer the one-to-one description as roles can be performed in structured group activities, case studies and simulations – situations that are far from one-to-one events. Neither am I fond of the term 'role play' itself: this seems to suggest a situation in which the learners are taking on an acting role, a completely different environment to a learning application. Certainly the learners enact roles that may be artificial, or different from their ordinary roles at work, but the aim should always be in training and development to make the learning event as real as possible – calling them role 'plays' leads the attitude in the other direction and suggests 'playing a game' rather than taking part in a serious learning event.

One-to-one interactions are normally used in providing skills practice in people learning programmes, where the practice is linked to learning related to such people skills as counselling, discipline, reprimand, recruitment, appraisal, selection, termination and grievance interviewing, and in which the two people take on the roles of interviewer and interviewee. 'One-to-one interactions' can be stretching the description a little in certain circumstances, such as in practice negotiations and selection/promotion panel interviews, in which frequently there are more than two people involved – for example, three interviewers and one interviewee in selection interviewing; and, say, three negotiators interacting with three other negotiators. I make no apology for these anomalies!

'Real-life' interviews

On training programmes these activities must perforce be artificial and contrived in the majority of cases. A nearer approach to real life is achieved by using actual workers as the interviewees, although this is a difficult arrangement administratively. I have used this approach in promotion interviewing training, with the interviewees rather than being other learners being people who have either recently attended such panels or are soon to do so. In the latter case, the training is helping them by giving them practice in being interviewed. Setting up similar situations for other one-to-one interactions such as counselling, grievance and so on is more difficult and the 'artificial' activity is probably the best that one can achieve. There are dangers in using 'real' people as the interviewees, in that the practice may become too real, with active emotions and unfortunate comments by the interviewer, and as a result the interviewee might be hurt. Obviously, interviewee selection must be careful in such cases and the interviewees thoroughly briefed.

Types of one-to-one interaction activities

The range of one-to-one interactions described above can be included in training programmes using:

- completely artificial role situations;
- real people situations replicated for the training programme;
- artificial role situations based on and modified from real situations to completely suit the training programme objectives.

In many ways, although the description appears to belie best practices, the artificial event offers the best learning opportunity. The situation and the roles can be constructed so that there is every opportunity for the range of skills learned to be practised, which is not always the case in real-life situations. The possible criticism by the learners is, however, based on the 'artificiality' and this can (and is) used as an excuse by the learners for less than excellent performance. If the situation can be described to the learners as having been taken from real cases, acceptance should be readier.

As in so many cases of skills learning, the initial learning is best achieved on a training programme which offers a protective environment for the newly discovered skills to be practised. At some time the learner will have to face a real person with a real problem, and if there has been practice in the safe learning environment, preferably on more than one occasion, the first real interview should not be as much of a shock as it would have been without a 'dummy run'. Consequently a training programme providing one-to-one interactions can offer:

- practice of learned skills in a safe or protected environment;
- rehearsal of additional, extended or different skills;
- exploration of behaviours, actions and events alien to the learners' norms or preferred approaches;
- rehearsal for a real event that is approaching.

Minimum brief interactions

Many one-to-one interactions are quite complex situations – after all life is like that – and a brief is required that gives a substantial amount of information to be assimilated for use during the interaction. However, extensive briefs are neither always necessary nor desirable, particularly where the learning group is at a mature, confident stage and willing to experiment and take risks. In such situations, minimal briefs might be used. These could simply state the situation and leave it to the participants to behave in a way that they think is appropriate, bearing in mind the interaction learning that has preceded this point in the programme.

The principal danger here is that the participants use the event as an opportunity to exhibit their acting prowess and take the situation over the top. Structured briefs require a minimum of acting and freewheeling; minimal briefs in fact tend to encourage these actions. The interaction should be prefaced by a warning about this danger and an encouragement for the participants to behave in as natural and normal manner as possible.

An example of an interaction in which this minimal briefing might be used is the stated situation where one of the participants has entered a shop with a complaint about an item recently purchased; the other takes the role of the shop manager who has been called to deal with the complaint, but has only that day had a difficult interview with the area manager about branches accepting complaints too easily.

Membership

In order to offer the maximum learning benefit, the opportunity for practice in all the one-to-one interaction situations must be given to all members of the learning group; they should not be restricted to one practice in one situation. The latter often happens when time is short in a programme covering a variety of people situations, or because of inflexible time restrictions, but compromises are always possible.

The most effective use of one-to-one interaction activities is to have all the group members practising the same situation at the same time. So, for example, when discipline interviewing is being practised in a training programme covering a wide range of interviewing situations, following input and perhaps structured group activities, all the members can be involved in practices in a format which allows them all to have at least one practice. The most effective approach for this is the triad method – this will be described fully later in this chapter.

Obviously when a number of interviewing groups are taking place at the same time the trainer cannot be with each group all the time. If the trainer feels his or her presence is essential, practice must be restricted so that one pair only at a time is in a one-to-one interaction so that feedback can be given by the trainer. This is very expensive in terms of the amount of time usually available within a programme, and can be avoided by using the learners themselves as the observers and reporters. The restricted approach also means that, unless a lot of time is used, learners usually have the opportunity for practice at one interview type only. If, however, this approach is the only one possible, in order to ensure that each learner has a practice opportunity, the instances should be included in the programme preparation. A matrix can be constructed matching the learners against the practice possibilities to ensure involvement without duplication and exclusion.

Timing

Consideration of timing involves two aspects – the timing position of the one-to-one interactions and the amount of time allocated to them. Apart from specially arranged rehearsals as described earlier, one-to-one interactions usually follow input sessions and other activities related to the particular skill in question. An input describing the techniques can be followed by simple interviews to practise such aspects as questioning, listening and so on. These would be followed by the one-to-one interactions themselves. Time for the first two activities will depend on the extent of the material involved, and the time allocated for the one-to-one interaction itself will usually depend on the complexity of the case. For practical purposes, to avoid excessive use of time in a programme and the full utilization of the learners, one-to-one interactions are usually planned to extend over a 20-minute period. The learners can either be informed that they have 20 minutes allocated for the interview, the interview can be stopped after 20 minutes (not a recommended action) or some flexibility introduced so that although the interview should only take 20 minutes it can be allowed to continue for five or ten minutes more. More time than this is normally not required, and remember that additional time given here may disrupt the timing of the remainder of your programme.

Time will also need to be allocated for review, whichever review method is used, and this requirement is frequently underestimated. This is particularly true if video recording is used with the one-to-one interactions although, as described in Chapter 5, there are approaches to minimize this.

Planning and design

In the same way that thorough preparation is required for all training programme activities, so it is for one-to-one interactions, as they can be complicated to obtain or produce, to run and to review. A suggested structure for your preparation might be:

1. Consider whether a one-to-one interaction is desirable, necessary or essential as part of the training programme; if so, decide that it should be included.
2. Identify the objectives for the interaction. These will normally be the learning points for the specific type of interaction involved, eg the structure and methods of a discipline interview and so on. These objectives must be as specific as possible and should be determinable from the content of the related input material.
3. Identify and obtain suitable one-to-one interactions for the programme. Many trainers and training departments have these interactions already available, usually customized to their particular organization. If necessary these can be modified according to changes in procedures, practices and attitudes. There is, however, a plethora of published collections of one-to-one interactions, some covering a range of interactions, others concentrating on specific types of interactions. These published interactions do not necessarily relate to your particular organization, but most can usually be easily modified.
4. Prepare the general situation brief and the specific briefs for the interviewer and the interviewee, with perhaps a combined brief for the observer. It is easy to say 'prepare the brief', but the actual practice is not as easy. If the brief is too long the learners will have difficulty in assimilating the material, however much preparation time is given; consequently the interaction may not succeed, or the learners who have not performed well may use this as an excuse for their performance. If it is too short essential information may be omitted and the interaction may suffer the same results. When you

are constructing a one-to-one interaction from scratch you should test out the briefs with a 'friendly' set of colleagues – not trainers, as they will view the brief from a completely different viewpoint to pseudo learners.

The observers should also be provided with an observation instrument and they too will be given time at the start of the interaction to familiarize themselves with this. The instrument can be a more complex one than for group activities as the observers will be concentrating on only two people, and in fact usually one at a time. Various instruments were discussed in Chapter 5.

5. In addition to the specific role briefs, the learners can usefully be given a list of rules for carrying out one-to-one interactions. If there is to be a series of interaction practices during a programme, this can be given near the start of the programme for reference throughout the event. An example of this is shown in Figure 11.1.

Rules for One-to-One Interactions

1. Read carefully the briefs that you have been given – you will be allowed sufficient time to read them and commit to memory all the information you need to perform your role effectively. The interaction will be fully effective if you can involve yourself in the role as fully and as naturally as possible, without further reference to the brief.

2. Use the time allocated fully and annotate your own comments on the briefing sheet. If there are parts of the brief you do not understand, ask now. The brief contains all the information you need to take part in the interview, although detail has been kept to a minimum to avoid overload.

3. Try, as you read the brief, to imagine yourself in this situation and how you would act and react, bearing in mind the techniques you will have learned for this specific type of interaction. Make provisional decisions about what you will do, but remember that you may have to be flexible within the role as the interaction progresses.

4. When you are in the interaction, be yourself as far as possible within the role, unless you have been specifically requested to behave in a different manner. Do not look on the event as an opportunity to act – you will find problems if you try to do this in a real interview! The role will give you the opportunity to use your existing or learned skills and you may find that you can call upon your prior experience to help you in the event.

5. Stick to the brief. Do not invent 'facts' other than those that would be natural in the circumstances. You may have to do this on occasions to supplement the brief information and to react to the other person, but any of these inclusions should be acceptable ones within the environment of the brief.

---

6. Follow the learning points relating to this type of situation as far as you are able. This is an opportunity for you to practise these skills in the 'safe' environment of the training programme before you have to interact in real life. Your organization may have different procedures or regulations than you are expected to follow – clear this with the trainer before starting the interaction.

7. Don't panic if your mind or memory goes. These interactions can be stressful. If you don't know what question to ask or what response to give and you are completely lost, don't be afraid to suggest an adjournment to let you get back on track. Often a minute or so only is necessary to let you organize your thoughts ready to resume the interview

Figure 11.1 *Rules for one-to-one interactions*

Usage

Method of running a one-to-one interaction

1. Allocate the pairs or other small groupings and identify for them the locations in which they will be interacting

2. Give information on how the interactions will run, be observed and reviewed – as suggested earlier, avoid the use of the words 'role play', using instead 'interaction', 'interview', 'meeting' or 'practice', whichever is the most relevant to the situation.

3. Ensure that the learners are clear about the rules summarized on the 'rules' sheet that they should have received.

4. Issue the briefs and the observer instruments. Give all participants time to read and assimilate the information and develop themselves into the relevant roles. Part of this period should be devoted to planning by both the interviewer and interviewee. The essence of interviewing, even under the more constrained environment of the training practice, is flexibility; but you can only be flexible if you have a base from which to work. The brief gives the basic information for the scene, it is up to the participants to fill in this information with live activity during the interaction.

    Suggest that the interviewer, having assimilated the brief:
    - considers the options for approaching the interaction;
    - considers the possible solution options for the apparent problem, but without closing their mind on one solution and appreciating that they may not be in possession of all the information;
    - decides how the interaction is to be opened: by a statement,

by a question, by an invitation to the interviewee to state the problem and so on;

- writes down their self-agreed opening contribution: the start of almost any event can be the most awkward and difficult stage; being fully prepared in this eases the entry;
- constructs a 'plan' of how they would like the interview to progress, always bearing in mind the need for complete flexibility, depending on the emergence of comments and responses from the interviewee.

Suggest that the interviewee completes a similar pre-interaction planning by:

- rehearsing a possible starting contribution or optional contributions depending on the approach made by the interviewer. This 'starter' may be a brief, impactive description of the problem, to the extent that they want this to emerge;
- deciding how they are going to react to the interviewer; fully open, open but with incomplete information until probed, reluctant to give information and so on;
- considering optional solutions to the problem, but keeping an open mind for a discussion of these solutions with the interviewer;
- considering a 'fall-back' position beyond which they will not go or accept.

5. Remind the learners that there is no 'right answer' for the situation, but that the purpose of the event is to let them practise the relevant skills and have an opportunity to experience this type of event if it is new to them, or to try different kinds of approaches.
6. Remind the participants how long they have to conduct the event, giving the time when the interaction should come to a close, rather than saying 'You have 20 minutes.'
7. Run the interaction. You will have decided on your role, depending on the number of subgroups, but the principal restriction for you is that you should not intervene during the interview unless everything has gone badly wrong, and particularly if your intervention is solicited by the participants. If there is a hiatus, remind the learners of the 'rule' that they can adjourn to sort out any problems of process themselves if possible.
8. Ensure that the interaction stops on time or determine how much more time each subgroup requires and whether this can be allowed within the programme time constraints. Sometimes, at the end of the allotted time, even though the interaction has not come to a final

result, it may have covered all the process points necessary. In this case you can stop the interaction, explaining to the participants why you are doing this. The principal point is that the practice is for the process, not the completion of the task, although completion of both may be desirable.

9. Let the participants come out of their roles. If the participants have really entered into the spirit of the interaction, they will have been 'living' the roles given to them and at the end of the interaction may still be in the role. Time must be given for them to wind down from what might have been an emotional or stressful event, ready for them to approach review in a rational manner. As suggested earlier, this can be achieved by giving them an instrument on which to record their reactions, thoughts, memories of events and so on, ready for the review. This period of reflection also acts as a tool to bring them out of the role and back to the learner role.

10. Sometimes the interaction has ended in frustration and the participants are highly charged emotionally. Even the completion of the reflection instrument may not bring them down from the 'high' and other techniques might have to be used. Some of these can include destressing activities, of which there are many, including:

   - writing down on a sheet of paper what is frustrating them, reading it out aloud then screwing up the sheet and throwing it away;
   - simply suggesting that the interaction is now over and that they might want to walk about for a few minutes; the physical act of walking can often relieve the stress;
   - holding the review session in another location, eg the interview room used by another pair of participants;
   - providing a number of empty cardboard boxes which they can destroy by jumping up and down on them: the physical activity either relieves the stress or they feel so foolish doing this that their stress disappears.

11. Review the interaction. The process for this will have been decided in the programme preparation period. Depending on the manner in which the practice has been set up, the participants may engage in a review and feedback with the trainer leading the activity, or the observers may take on this role with the learners they have been observing. In this case the observers will need to have been given some instruction and/or support prior to the practice in how to conduct the review. After a period of subgroup reviews all the participants can return to a main plenary to raise and discuss significant points that may have arisen in all interactions.

12. If the interaction has been recorded on video, the recording should be used in the review, a variety of options being available.

   – If the review is held with a singular pair of interviewer and interviewee, selected parts of the recording can be used with verbal feedback on incidents, behaviours and reactions observed – anticipate that this will take considerably longer than a purely verbal review.
   – Another approach might be to send the subgroups away to view the full recording before returning for a review session, either in plenary or with their observer.
   – A verbal review might be held, but with the offer of the availability of the videos and equipment during the evening when the participants might wish to view their interactions – this is particularly useful when time is at a premium, although there may be some resistance as you are using their time.
   – If single interviews are held, one after the other, with the full group observing, participants in the previous interaction can be excused from the next interaction and can view the video of their event in a separate room. A verbal resumé can follow this viewing, back in the plenary session, with the participants having identified significant events and techniques.

13. The final activity in the event, following the review and feedback session of whatever nature, should be relating of the process of the interaction and the lessons learned to the 'back at work' situation. Instances of practice can be sought from the learners and their views encouraged about how they see their practice being changed when they return. This action planning can be linked with the final processes of the review, this being completed by a summary of the learning points on a posted flipchart sheet to which 'real-life' comments are added in this final discussion.

FEEDBACK GROUNDRULES

Some groundrules to help you make the review and feedback sessions as effective as possible include:

■ Give as much positive feedback as possible – 'Such and such was an effective move', 'Keep on doing so-and-so.'
■ Suggest rather than prescribe. A more acceptable and constructive feedback, rather than 'Do this and you will do better' is to say 'You

may like to try so and so. I've seen that work for a lot of people in this situation.'

- Don't make the feedback negative – rather than say 'That's not the way to do it', try 'How about trying it such and such a way?'.
- Give the feedback as soon as possible after the event – the longer the gap, the less effective it becomes. You will have to be careful about this aspect when using video recordings as deferred feedback instruments.
- Focus the feedback on how you saw it, rather than involving others. 'I saw you do so and so...', not 'The observers/group will have seen you...'
- Be factual rather than judgemental – comment on what was seen, not what you interpreted from what happened; let them do the interpretation when you have reported the event.

Two people or groups are involved in feedback – the person giving the feedback and the person receiving the feedback. It can be difficult to receive feedback, so some groundrules for this include:

- Listen to the feedback in an active manner, rather than just hear it, and consequently you are receiving it.
- Listen carefully; there may be nuances that tell you more than the apparently direct comments.
- Try to avoid being defensive – remember that most people like to give feedback and they do so with a (sometimes misguided) impression that they are helping you.
- Avoid rationalizing your actions and behaviour to avoid accepting the feedback from others who may have seen the real effect.
- Be open minded.
- Remember that feedback can represent the views of one person only – seek feedback if possible from more than one person and balance what you receive.
- Check your understanding of what has been said to you by asking questions of the giver of the feedback.
- Having received the feedback, take time out (even a short period) and carefully evaluate the accuracy and potential of what has been said.
- In accepting the feedback, consider how you can use it to help you to improve.

THE TRIAD APPROACH

Triads and the triad approach to interviews and observation have been mentioned several times. In addition to meaning simply a group of three people, the term has a specific meaning in interview training. The stages of the triad approach include:

1. Divide the learning group into subgroups, each containing three people.
2. Identify the three people as A, B and C.
3. Request A to take on the role of interviewer in the first interview, B to be the interviewee and C to be the observer. In the second interview of three C will become the interviewer, A the interviewee and B the observer. In the third interview B becomes the interviewer, C the interviewee and A the observer. In this way all three participants will have the opportunity to take on all three roles within their subgroup.
4. Issue the relevant briefs for all the activities and allocate time for the briefs for the first interaction to be studied and assimilated. Between the first and second interviews and the second and third interviews the relevant briefs can be studied prior to the enactment of the interviews. As an alternative, only the first interview briefs can be issued initially, subsequent ones being issued by you when you are told by the triad that they are ready for them.
5. In their separate rooms, the triads enact the interactions. In the first event A interviews B according to the brief and C observes the interaction (without any intervention whatsoever). At the end of the allotted time for the interaction C conducts a review and feedback session, again for an allotted time, with A and B. C should follow the observation and feedback guidelines detailed earlier – behaviours, statements, actions and reactions should be noted during the interaction in addition to noting the interviewer's use of the relevant techniques; the review should follow a pattern of:

   (a) how the interviewer saw the interactions and his or her actions, etc;
   (b) how the interviewee saw the interaction and any points they wish to raise about the actions and behaviour of the interviewer and their reactions to these;
   (c) and finally how the observer saw any additional aspects or divergences from the interviewer's and interviewee's perceptions.

The observer should be advised to keep discussion about the task to the minimum except where it links with particular actions and behaviours. Even so, this review period can take up a considerable time if not controlled discretely by the trainer, who should try to visit each group to ensure that everybody has a chance to say something.

6. The action is repeated with the second and third interviews, and as a final review the full group comes together in plenary to discuss any general and significant points that have emerged from their separate discussions.

Because there are three successive interviews and their review periods, this approach is quite expensive in terms of time, but it does ensure that everybody has a chance at a particular type of interaction and that the processes are reviewed at peer level. You must accept that you have principally a monitoring role, ensuring that the process is operating correctly, problems are resolved and, if necessary, timing is strictly adhered to.

GUIDELINES FOR THE REVIEW SESSION FOLLOWING THE ACTIVITY

Some of the aspects you might investigate in the review session following this activity include:

Questions to the interviewer

- How did you feel when you realized the implications of your brief?
- What form did your pre-interview planning take? What were your objectives?
- What type of approach did you plan to use for the interview?
- How did you feel immediately before the start of the interview?
- To what extent did you follow your plan during the interview?
- How do you feel you were able to get the message over to the interviewee?
- How do you feel the interviewee reacted to the interview?
- How appropriate do you feel your behaviours were during the interview?
- How do you feel about the outcome of the interview?
- What do you think the interviewee feels about this outcome?
- How difficult was the interview?
- Any other comments?

Questions to the interviewee

- How did you feel when you realized the implications of your brief?
- What form did your pre-interview planning take? What were your objectives?

- What type of approach did you plan to use for the interview?
- How did you feel immediately before the start of the interview?
- How did you feel when the interviewer told you the reason for the interview?
- What were your feelings and reactions during the interview?
- How did you feel you were treated by the interviewer?
- Were there any occasions you can recall when the interviewer's behaviours were not appropriate?
- How appropriate do you feel your behaviours were during the interview?
- How do you feel about the outcome of the interview?
- What do you think the interviewer feels about this outcome?
- How difficult was the interview?
- Any other comments?

Similar questions relating to both the interviewer and interviewee should be asked of the observer, or the observer should use them in his or her part of the review when this form of review is used.

VARIATIONS

A number of variations on the basic process of interactions are possible, usually to ensure that specific or additional points are made. Some are more risky than others and should only be attempted if you feel sufficiently capable of dealing with whatever might result. Many of the variations fall into what is usually described as psychodrama and, as they are manipulations of the process and the people, should not be entered into lightly.

Doubling

Doubling, or ghosting as it is sometimes called, is the technique used when participants other than the original role players take part in the interaction, but usually only for a temporary period. The 'doubler' steps into the interaction at a particular point and for a particular reason and takes over the part of the interviewer or interviewee (usually the former). The doubler might in fact be the trainer, but whoever is involved the doubling must be performed skilfully and with care.

Doubling is most frequently used when, during the course of an interaction, either the interviewer or interviewee (or another role) seems to lose their way and does not know what to say next. The intended doubler must be absolutely certain that the hiatus has occurred and that the participants will not be able to extricate themselves. This is part of the risk involved in this technique, as if an intervention is made too quickly the tenor of the interview might be upset and problems, rather than support, caused for the participant.

When it is certain that the interview is in danger of premature termination because of difficulties being experienced by one of the participants, the doubler goes to stand behind the person, touches them on the shoulder to let them know they are there, and makes the contribution they think should be made to continue the interaction. This intervention might need one or two contributions before the doubler can step back and let the original participant continue. Hopefully, the original participant will have recovered to the extent that they can continue, otherwise the interaction should be brought to a close and a discussion held on what had happened, why it had occurred and how it could have been avoided or resolved.

The major risk of this type of intervention is that the person on whom the intervention has been made resents the action, either immediately, with unfortunate results, or expressed later in the review. I have had experiences in which, during the review, the observer said of an intervention in this manner that if it happened to them they would resent it. The interviewee on each occasion said, however, that they experienced nothing but relief at being helped out of a problem situation, and as the interview then proceeded they learned a lot that would not have happened if the intervention had not been made.

The risks, however, are very real and it may be helpful to discuss the technique early in the programme and obtain the agreement of the learners that doubling might take place from time to time.

An alternative use of doubling is the deliberate replacement of the initial interviewer or interviewee at stages in the interview. When the doubler intervenes, they then take the participant's place until they too might be doubled according to a prearranged plan or at a signal from the trainer. This gives more learners the opportunity to take part in interactions, to bring rather different approaches to the situation and to appreciate different points of views and approaches. There is much less risk of resentment against intervention if this plan is agreed and followed. This alternative can also help the shyer members who would like to take part but would draw back from doubling voluntarily.

Role reversal

Role reversal can be a novel way of achieving learning, particularly where a real situation is used for the interaction or the participants can relate easily to the roles required. Normally when you have a problem you are too involved to consider it rationally and your emotions can get in the way of making positive decisions. If an interaction is viewed in this way, similar problems arise in stopping the participant from seeing the problems clearly. The technique is based on the frequent comment 'If only they could have seen the problem from my point of view'. Role reversal helps to do just that.

Two methods of the technique are available. The first uses an interaction situation where the participants can identify with the role or the situation. For example, where one of the learners has previously had to conduct a discipline interview or will soon have to do so, in the interaction they will take the part of the person being disciplined. This reversal will help them to obtain an insight of the viewpoint of the person on the receiving end of the interview. Consequently, this should help them in the real situation to appreciate what is happening in the mind of the person being disciplined and to modify their approach accordingly. If such real situations are approaching, the interaction should be designed to be as close as possible to the real situation – the learners themselves can supply the information necessary to produce the interaction activity.

The second approach is for the role play to start off normally with the problem owner taking their real-life part – again this works more effectively with real-life problems translated into interaction activities. At a critical stage of the interview, which will have been proceeding normally and hopefully according to the plan of the interviewer, the trainer asks the two participants to reverse roles and take up the interaction at the point of the switchover. As the participants have to take each other's parts and therefore attitude from this point, the problem owner has to argue from a different point of view than would have been their normal approach, and so see another aspect of the situation. It is usual for the participants to carry on the arguments that were being made before the reversal, and on many occasions observers can see realization appear on the learners' faces when they see that there is another, perhaps more appropriate viewpoint.

The reversal consequently helps everybody to see and perhaps appreciate other people's points of view and that there is usually more than one point of view and therefore more potential solutions that can be considered.

Possible problems can be avoided by the trainer in the second approach being very sensitive to the stage at which the reversing is suggested. Of course, this can be avoided by using the first approach, although this may not be the most relevant technique.

The empty chair

One-to-one interaction training owes many of its techniques and methods to psychology and therapy approaches. The 'empty chair' is one of these and is often used generally to take pressure off a person who wants to release the feelings produced by a problem ownership. In traditional one-to-one interaction activities, as the title implies, two people need to be involved – the interviewer and the interviewee – and frequently this produces an element of artificiality. Even when a real problem is used, usually only one of the participants has the problem as a real one, the other person having to take an artificial role.

The empty chair or monodrama resolves many of these problems, but should only be used at a stage in the training programme when the atmosphere has developed into an open and trusting one, and one in which the learners are willing to do something different and perhaps take some risks in the exposure of deep feelings.

The basic approach in this technique is to have two chairs facing each other; the problem owner sits in one and the other remains empty. When the problem owner feels ready to do so, they start to describe the problem to a 'person' in the empty chair. Because there is no chance of interruptions or disagreement by the 'other person' the problem owner can describe the problem in detail and to whatever depth they feel able to do – usually this increases as the problem owner settles into the activity and feels more comfortable and able to allow these deeper feelings to emerge. Quite frequently the speaker becomes so immersed in the situation that they forget there is nobody opposite them and speak as if the empty chair was occupied.

The method is based on the model that if you talk about your problem sufficiently it is very likely that you will lead yourself to your own solutions. This occurs frequently in the empty chair activity. At the very least the problem owner has been given the opportunity to air the problem with which they are concerned, without the complication of other people, and even this can produce an easing of the problem. Sometimes the problem owner comes to the conclusion that there is either no problem or it is so minor that they are wasting their time being concerned about it.

A variation of the approach described above requires more activity and action by the person taking part in the 'interaction'. This variation starts in a similar way, with the problem owner starting to describe the problem to the empty chair. When this initial phase is under way the speaker moves over to the empty chair and asks questions, raises objections or makes comments as if they were the permanent responder in an interaction. The speaker then moves back to the original chair and responds to their own questions etc. If the problem owner finds that they are able to continue in this way and, although it seems to be an unnatural process, most do find they can deal with it, the switching continues until the problem has been talked through.

Psychodrama or 'hot role play'

This type of interaction again works best with real-life problems brought to the programme with the learners wanting to release their feelings and hopefully resolve the problems. The basis of the technique is that the problem owner relives the problem, but away from the real environment of the problem and in the safer and more supportive atmosphere of the training programme. In many cases it is necessary for the trainer or facilitator, who should be skilled and experienced in this type of approach, to take part in the interaction with the problem owner – rather than one of the other learners.

The skilled facilitator can help the problem owners through the process by enabling them to relive the problem as far as possible in as realistic manner as possible. The facilitator may have to take on the role of the other person in the problem to do this. The problem owner can move into a highly emotive state, which can be dangerous if the facilitator is not skilled in therapy methods.

The most natural 'hot interaction' is when an issue arises in the here and now of the training programme and the issue is used as a basis for the interaction. Frequently this comes about from a problem arising between two learners on the programme and the problem is worked through there and then to (a) solve the problem and (b) give the participants the opportunity to practise real interactive skills. When the problem arises the trainer/facilitator invites the participants to sit down and talk the problem through in front of the group, having obtained agreement for this 'public' exposure. The rest of the group often asks that it be enacted in front of them as they (a) want to experience the type of interaction for their own future possible needs and (b) observe how the participants handle the situation.

It can often help if before the start of the interaction some ground-rules are suggested and agreed, such as the non-overpersonal comments by one participant to or about the other; a minimum of interruption and agreement that they should each give each other a full opportunity to have their say; that permission is given to the trainer to intervene if it is felt that the interaction is moving beyond acceptable bounds. The setting of rules may seem to make the event very formal, but in my experience if the participants feel they own the rules they restrain the participants to a realistic interaction, not without emotion but without negative emotional behaviours.

The presence of the group may slow down the interaction at the start, but once the participants, perhaps with a little support by the facilitator, become more deeply involved in the interaction, it can develop into a very natural event. A number of developments can take place as this type of interaction progresses – the trainer and/or the group can in fact be brought into the interaction by the two participants themselves with the result that a 'family' counselling session develops.

MONITORING

The trainer, although the role may not be overtly active, has a major role in one-to-one interaction activities. They must constantly be aware of the emotional atmosphere existing in the interactions and be prepared, once they are convinced of the position, to step in to avoid damage being done to the participants.

The other area in which the trainer can support the learning is in the review and feedback sessions. Although he or she may not be 'actively' involved in these reviews, a watching brief should be to ensure that the maximum benefit is obtained from such sessions. The review sessions have enormous potential for learning – frequently much more than the event itself – and the trainer has the responsibility to ensure that this is fulfilled. You will find that most people like to give feedback – solicited or unsolicited – although there is not the same reaction to receiving feedback. If the feedback given conflicts with what they see about their own actions, feelings or behaviours they will become defensive and reject the feedback. The trainer has a major role in ensuring, either by observer support or even a training event early in the programme, that the feedback is given in the most acceptable form possible, so that it supports and enhances the learning rather than becoming a source of conflict. Reread the feedback groundrules given earlier in this chapter.

12
—

Experiential Interactive Learning and Activities

Experiential activities are difficult to classify and describe in my rather arbitrary method of titling different forms of activity, other than as an extended description of practical activities. I see them as usually short (although this is not a requirement), generally informal and to some extent unstructured activities performed within groups. These groups are usually small and occur in training and development programmes where the emphasis is on the development of interpersonal or interactive skills and behaviour, rather than on technically applied skills. In a rather similar way to the structured group activities described in Chapter 9, they concentrate on behaviours and feelings, but with a stronger emphasis on these aspects, and enable participants to assess the manner in which they relate to other people, the remainder of the group acting as a sounding board and reflector of these behaviours.

Managers and other practitioners tend to concentrate their attention of what they do in terms of the tasks for which they are responsible, taking notice of their behaviour and its effects on themselves and others as a secondary aspect. Training and development programmes attempt to interlink these two aspects of performance by demonstrating that, in order to perform a task effectively, the needs and feelings of others must be taken into account. Interpersonal and interactive programmes tend to place the emphasis on the people relationship aspect, suggesting that if effective relationships are developed with people's bosses, peers and staff, the effective completion of the task is achieved more readily. Consequently, training programmes of this nature require and encourage the participants to develop and share their feelings and emotions, rather than hide these in front of others, and experiential activities are designed to support the emergence of these attitudes.

WHY USE EXPERIENTIAL ACTIVITIES AND APPROACHES?

- Learners are invited to develop their communication and interpersonal skills and so become more able to ensure the successful performance of tasks when working with others;
- open interaction increases the self-awareness of the individual and their awareness of the behaviour and needs of others;
- wider considerations of problems, particularly those involving people;
- opportunities to examine personal behaviours and practise modification of these behaviours;
- development of trust between people, particularly when working in a team;
- the rare opportunity to receive real, open and honest feedback about how you are seen by others and how they react to you;
- another rare opportunity to discharge your feelings in a safe environment;
- realization that you are not alone and that others have the same failings as yourself, enjoy or otherwise the same sorts of feelings, and that something can be done.

WHEN TO USE EXPERIENTIAL ACTIVITIES AND APPROACHES

The interpersonal, experiential approaches and activities described in this chapter have a variety of uses and can be introduced in a variety of situations. They can and are used in:

- complete interpersonal and interactive skills learning programmes, concerned solely with the learners' behaviours, relationship skills and behavioural awareness – of self and others;
- learning programmes where structured, task-oriented experiences are included but restrict the wider appreciation and learning of the participants;
- when trust has developed in a learning group and there is a high degree of group and individual support existing;
- training programmes related to learning methods and techniques;
- trainer development programmes – to widen the knowledge and skills bases of the learner–trainers for more effective programme production.

INTERACTIVE PROGRAMME MODELLING

Most of the interpersonal programmes are based on a personal development model of some nature – Maslow's Hierarchy of Needs; Berne's Transactional Analysis; McGregor's Theories X and Y; the psychologies of Skinner, Freud and Jung; Honey's BMod and FMod (behaviour modification and feelings modification); and the perception and awareness model developed by Luft and Ingram (the Johari Window), to name some of the models favoured by different practitioners.

The T-Group approach

The trainers involved in programmes of this nature are usually referred to as 'facilitators' as in this type of programme the teaching/training/input content of the trainer is at a minimum, learning being supported or facilitated. The facilitator is present to act as a resource to the learners, to provide vehicles for their activities as and when necessary, to be the expert witness when this is required by the learners and to help the learners develop their own learning by providing an environment supportive to this end. The extreme examples of this type of approach are demonstrated in what are known as T-Groups, Sensitivity Groups, Encounter Groups and Laboratory Training. 'T-Groups' derives from the 'Training Group', an approach to human relations training developed from the small groups discussion approach of Kurt Lewin in the 1940s and further developed in a training approach at the National Training Laboratories in the USA. The philosophy of T-Group training includes:

- real learning comes from experiencing real situations, albeit in a training environment, rather than from the artificiality of constructed activities;
- learning will only be achieved through honest feedback within the group;
- the 'here and now' of what is happening in the group, particularly in relation to feelings, is of the highest importance, rather than the actions required to perform a task;
- learning will be achieved whatever the event might be that is occurring, provided that the atmosphere is conducive to the sought learning.

In order to satisfy this philosophy, the resulting objectives are stated as, to increase:

- the sensitivity and awareness of the participants to their own feelings and reactions, and those of others;
- the ability of individuals and the group to analyze and assess what is happening within the group and between individuals;
- the participants' skills in adopting new behaviours and adapting existing behaviours so that the appropriate behaviour pattern is adopted, feedback can be given and received with sensitivity and feelings can be controlled.

Within a T-Group there is an atmosphere of dual roles in which all the group members participate in activities but observe fully at the same time. Every encouragement is given for them to raise immediately any issue that might result from the activity or actions of the group or individuals – pleasure, concern, anger, sorrow, rejection – and have these explored fully within the group. The facilitator may, in a supportive, resourcing role, offer activities for the group to use as a vehicle to satisfy their objectives, but normally the group develops its own activities that relate to the way the group is developing and what it wants to emerge. The facilitator may again provide resources and activities to help this development, but the control of the group is almost completely in the hands of the group itself.

T-Groups may start in an almost traditional way because the facilitator is working to a model that suggests that the learners will settle in and develop more easily if the programme progresses from the known and to the unknown. The facilitator has to develop a strong sense of awareness and sensitivity in order to be able to identify when to start withdrawing from an active role.

There are alternative, almost completely unstructured approaches in which the group is left to its own devices from the start and the only involvement of a facilitator is to encourage them to take steps to develop their relationships and learning.

Whether the programme is structured, semi-structured or completely unstructured, the group development is almost forecastable, following a five-stage model for group development which suggests that most groups go through five steps in a progressive manner. The speed at which the group proceeds through the stages will depend on a variety of complex factors – remember we are dealing with people – and in fact some groups may not move beyond certain stages. The groups formed in this way are not necessarily stable, particularly when external changes are introduced – new members are introduced or support from management is withdrawn – or when internal factors start to influence the group – mini-retrogressions as a result of conflict between some individuals, a desire/need for power by an individual, jealousies that are normal to people in groups and so on.

The stages are frequently described as:

- forming
- storming
- norming
- performing
- mourning.

In the 'forming' stage the group has just come together, individuals may be strangers to each other and there are feelings (which they may attempt to hide) of uncertainty, apprehension, excitement, enthusiasm, distrust, interest. It is at this stage that introductory activities and icebreakers can usefully be introduced. When the group tries to develop it enters the 'storming' stage, but because the individuals have not moved completely away from their (principally hidden) feelings of distrust and suspicion, conflict and even minor aggression can arise as a result of challenges – usually concerning power. Members may decide to opt out or even walk out and the general atmosphere is one of anxiety. The facilitator must be sensitive in his or her interventions at this stage, but can facilitate movement by offering – not enforcing – suggestions for activity which will progressively lead to the greater sharing of positive and helpful feelings and the reduction of the negative feelings existing at the start of the stage.

If the group is handled or handles itself with sensitivity and increasing openness it moves to the 'norming' stage, when agreements are reached (perhaps through compromise), group and interactive skills start to develop and conscious or unconscious contracting takes place. 'Rules', determined by the group, are agreed and operated, procedures start to become the norm and help the stability of the group and differences of opinion tend to be resolved more by negotiation than power approaches. The 'performing' stage is the development of norming when the group performs whatever it is expected to or wants to achieve. This stage continues with the fluctuations mentioned above, in which the group can jump backwards and forwards between stages – even returning to the forming stage in extreme circumstances – until the time comes for the group to disband, the 'mourning' stage.

If this staged model is applied to the experiential group it is suggested that in the forming stage the structured group activities are the more useful and acceptable ones; in the storming stage there can be a development from the structured approaches to much more unstructured, group-developed activities. Norming and performing are demonstrated by the responsibility of the group for what they do to achieve their objectives, calling on the facilitator as a resource when necessary. At the mourning stage the activity can again be a mixture of structured activities (to ensure a clean break with intentions of learning implementation) and informal, unstructured closing activities, although sometimes a group welcomes a formal activity to do this and so ease the sadness, regrets or anti-climatic feelings of this stage.

The Johari Window

Many interpersonal skills programmes are seen as instruments to provide maximum movement of behaviour through feedback – preferably informal, agreed feedback between the members of the group. The facilitator can support this by feedback of observations using Behaviour Analysis, and this approach often provides an anchor on which more personal, inter-feedback can develop.

A model which demonstrates the value of personal feedback is provided by the Johari Window. This is a model of perception and awareness developed by two Americans, Joseph Luft, a psychologist and Harry Ingram, a psychiatrist, and their names have been used to form the unusual title – Jo and Hari to form Johari. The 'Window' part of the model's title reflects the basis for the model in that a window exists that reflects the various aspects of a person's behaviour. It is a two-way window in which information flows out from us to others, voluntarily or otherwise, and inwards from others as feedback. As a result of this movement we should be able to share more with others and consequently encourage them to share more with us – a mutual increase of behaviour awareness and action.

The Window has four panes, as shown in Figure 12.1, each pane representing knowledge and awareness at different levels of perception. The panes will not be of equal size from one person to another and each individual's Window is capable of being modified as the result of an increase in group trust, the outward sharing of feelings and the inward statement of feedback of perception.

The top left pane is known as the Arena and contains what you know about yourself and what others see about you. It is the area of open and public knowledge that the owner is happy to share. The size of this pane varies considerably with the individual, their openness and their willingness to expose themselves.

	Known to self	Not known to self
Known to others	ARENA	BLIND SPOT
Not known to others	FACADE	UNKNOWN

Figure 12.1 *The Johari Window*

The bottom left pane contains information that it is known to yourself, but as far as others are concerned the image presented will be the one you want to project. Consequently others are unaware of the real image. The Facade is clearly related to the various acts or roles we perform in public, roles we want others to see as the real us. The ability we have in acting roles determines to what extent the Facade is maintained, or whether our act is seen through and the awareness really returns to the Arena. Often our Facade is maintained from what may be a false sense of security, the individual being afraid of revealing their true self, because if they do they may suffer emotionally – 'People may not like me if they see me as I really am.'

The top right pane is the reverse of the Facade and contains knowledge about you known to others but of which you are unaware. It is common for others to see aspects of our behaviour of which we are unaware, and we remain so unless we are told about them. If the level of openness between ourselves and others is acceptable, this feedback will take place; in consequence the Blind Spot area will reduce to our benefit and the Arena will increase as we gain information we did not previously hold.

The bottom right pane is thought to exist in us all; areas of 'us' about which nobody is aware, including ourselves. Some of these aspects may be so deeply hidden that they never emerge, but others may be just lurking underneath the psychological surface and with appropriate stimuli may come to light.

Movement of the panes of the Johari Window can be the result of and demonstrate the development of a group or individual. At the beginning of a group's life the Arena pane will be small, as few members will be willing to disclose much about themselves. To counterbalance the reduced Arena, the Facade will be enlarged as we perform an act, showing an image of ourselves that we wish to project and which may not be real. No feedback is being given so the Blind Spot remains the same, as does the Unknown area. With increasing openness and feedback as the group moves through storming, norming and performing, the Facade and Blind Spot reduce in size, awareness moving into the Arena, giving aspects of the Unknown area the opportunity to emerge.

Activities designed to encourage open feedback will be used in the programme to achieve these Window movements.

Timing

The timing of activities in interpersonal programmes is one of the most difficult areas for the trainer, indeed the timing of the event itself has similar major problems. The early structured activities present few problems, but this state may not last for any length of time. The objective is to transfer formality to informality, power from the facilitator to the group, and with this transfer the facilitator's control of time reduces and may eventually disappear. The only feasible method of controlling this aspect in any way is to ensure that as power is transferred to the group responsibilities are also transferred, one of them being the need to achieve certain objectives within a constrained period of time – the period of the programme up to the time the facilitator has to regain control to end the event in an effective manner. However, even this may be left to the group if it is reaching a sufficient level of maturity and responsibility to take appropriate and effective action itself.

Preparation and design

Although many of the activities taking place in programmes involving the use of many experiential activities are spontaneous or learner generated, this should not suggest that preparation for such an event is not necessary. In fact the reverse is the case. The facilitators must:

1. Determine the approaches they will take.
2. Consider the extent and type of interventions they can plan.
3. Identify and prepare for the use of structured activities at the beginning and end of the event, semi-structured activities at other times, and produce a list of 'spontaneous' ideas that can be suggested to the learners if advice is sought.
4. Determine how time will be 'controlled'.
5. Decide on the use of observation techniques such as Behaviour Analysis and the use to which they may be put if required.
6. Decide on a role that they can follow, but with a flexible attitude for change depending on circumstances that arise.

Because you will not know the exact form that the event will follow (this path being determined to a major extent by the learners), you will need to collect a large reservoir of resources – structured and semi-structured activities, ideas for 'spontaneous' activities, instruments for observation, reflection and feedback. The initial structured activities you intend to use should be non-threatening, but in a form that will indicate the need for the learners to be more open in their views and feelings, and with discrete guidance being given to the learners on how to review and feed back activities in the way these initial activities are reviewed.

HOW I SEE MYSELF

After an appropriate introductions activity and introduction to the programme, a useful bridging activity is to seek further and more personal information about the learners than would emerge during a normal introduction activity. It does not guarantee that deep feelings and attitudes will emerge, but my experience is that the learners are quite keen to talk about themselves and welcome specific subjects on which to speak.

This activity is introduced by the facilitator in terms of a method of progressing the action of the group to develop their knowledge of each other and start building a group relationship.

1. Issue the briefing form shown in Figure 12.2.
2. Give the participants time to reflect on the form, complete the open parts of the statements and rehearse their presentations.
3. The learning group, if small in size (say six members) can stay in the one group; if larger (say 12 members) two groups can be formed.
4. Within whatever grouping is decided, the learners present to the remainder their responses and why they have made these responses. No pressure, other than encouragement, should be placed on the learners to express deeper feelings and attitudes than it appears they wish to do.
5. Following the presentations the facilitator can lead a discussion about the activity, seeking the views of the learners on how they felt about the questions and about what they were expected to say; how they felt about what they said and what others said; whether, if they were to repeat the activity, they would behave in any different way; to what extent they feel the activity has progressed the group relationship.
6. If sub-groups are used, after the sub-group presentations a co-facilitator could lead the discussion with one of the groups while you lead the other. After these sub-group reviews, the learners can come together in the full group to comment on general significant points that emerged.

As I See Myself

1. Back home my family sees me...

2. Back on the job, my colleagues see me ....

3. I think my boss sees me as ....

4. When people talk about high achievers I would say that I ....

5. My greatest need as a manager/supervisor (whatever) is ....

6. I feel happiest when ....

7. I feel most alone when ....

8. What I feel most disappointed about in my life is ....

9. With respect to being candid, open or 'levelling' with people I ....

10. As a group member I usually ....

11. The feelings (emotions) I can express most easily are ....

12. The feelings (emotions) I find most difficult to express are ....

13. My first impression of this group is ....

14. When I receive bad feedback about my actions or behaviour I ....

15. I came on this course because ....

16. I hope to get .... out of this course

Figure 12.2 *Self-disclosure briefing sheet*

Activities following early structured ones, to encourage self-disclosure and openness, can be progressively less structured and prescriptive, with the aim being development to a completely unstructured, informal and spontaneous programme culture. In this phase, the learners will take over the control of and responsibility for most of their own learning. Certainly, at the earliest opportunity, even in the more structured part of the event, the learners should be given full responsibility, perhaps following initial guidance and preferably by example, of conducting reviews of actions and activities and giving feedback in an effective manner.

If at later stages in the event the facilitator, as a resource, is asked to provide activities for the group to perform, these should be restricted to minimally imposed structure types and might simply be the barest of headings and briefing. An example of such an experiential activity might be suggesting that the group consider, using all the information at their disposal, 'Where are we now?'. Similar developmental and experiential events could be suggesting that they consider 'Behaviour modification by bargaining and horse-trading. How would the group go about this and how successful might it be?'. The principal purposes of these suggestions are to continue the development of the group in their ability to work together as a team to solve problems that affect them all, to enable them to practise and improve their behaviour both as individuals and as a group entity, and to provide behavioural experiences from which they can learn and develop.

THE RESOURCE BOX

My general suggestions so far in the introduction of experiential activities or any other activity that supports an experiential learning culture is that the facilitator has a role that becomes less and less evident as time progresses. Early actions set the group on the path to mutual development by means of non-threatening, more or less structured activities, moving through less and less structure and prescription to a learner-centred situation. My experience is that even when this latter stage has been reached, because the learning can be at times traumatic and new to the learners, they still seek support from the facilitator. This is obviously acceptable when it is solicited. But the facilitator must not use invitations to support as a means of regaining power and control, offering only the minimum help to act as a trigger for the group's regaining their own salvation.

To this end, during the facilitator's preparation for the programme, a resource box might be constructed. This is in fact a large box full of folders and other resources. The folders contain the descriptions, instructions and briefs for a large number of relevant activities, ranging from the structured through semi-structured to the simply expressed but revealing unstructured activities of the types suggested above. All the materials necessary to perform the activities should also be available, although many of the folders will contain only a sheet of paper with questions similar to those posed above about the position of the group or its attitude to behaviour modification.

The facilitator's response to a request for intervention might simply be to refer them to the box to choose something that fits their current needs – this act in itself is a developmental activity in assessment, analysis and decision-making, and can be as major as many complex structured activities! You can inform them, implicitly or explicitly, that the choice to use or not use them, the choice to make and the decision about how to use them would be theirs, but you would, as always, be available to provide any information, resource or support they might need.

BEHAVIOUR ANALYSIS FEEDBACK

One of the opportunities provided for you as a non-intervening facilitator is that for large periods of time you have the chance to observe the group closely and analyze their behaviour, perhaps using Behaviour Analysis. It is always useful to let the group know early on that this is what you will be doing, what BA is and how it might eventually be used. Few groups object to you doing this and in fact become very interested in the possible results. My practice has been to resist letting them have information too soon, on the basis that one swallow does not make summer, rather collecting and summarizing data until, about two-thirds of the way through the event, the offer of BA feedback can be made. This offer is rarely refused. Summarized in some detail the data will show their behaviour patterns during the period and how these might have modified. Accepted research data can also be provided with the BA material in easily interpreted format and the group presented with the material to assess and analyze in terms of individual and group behaviour patterns. I say very little about the material other than explaining the format, but again am always available for clarification questions. Allow plenty of time for the group to examine their analysis sheets as individuals, to voluntarily compare their data with other members of the group either in pairs (usually initially) or (subsequently) in open group and to identify:

- their behaviour patterns;
- behaviours they feel they need to modify in some way.

Depending on the awareness of the group, you may or may not need to intervene to suggest this modification of behaviour patterns (individual and/or group) and also to support them in deciding on the most appropriate ways to achieve these. The next activity, structured or unstructured, should include an objective of practice of modified behaviour and particular feedback on the success of this modification. I have frequently found a fishbowl activity valuable for this purpose, although almost any activity will give them the opportunity to aim for their modification objectives.

EGO

At the behaviour modification stage, or perhaps earlier if group movement is particularly slow or is being retarded, the introduction of the Ego rule can be suggested. Certainly in the forming and storming, and often in the norming stages, the learners make comments about 'People say that...', 'They seem to think that...', or even 'One can always try...'. These are usually attempts to depersonalize suggestions or statements, frequently because the contributor is afraid of being challenged if the suggestion comes out as a very personally desired one. Personal generalizations of this nature tend to keep the group in a more formal, 'at arm's length' atmosphere which is not conducive to the development of relationships and the progress of the group. In many cases the group is aware that something is holding them back, and if depersonalization is one of the factors they are usually happy for you to intervene, although the timing for this must be right. Most people are taught that too great a use of the word 'I' is not socially acceptable, and find it difficult to use even in interpersonal situations. They are often relieved when the 'rules' are amended so that, rather than being discouraged, they are encouraged to be egoistic.

Intervention by the facilitator has to be discrete and the six-category intervention analysis of Heron, referred to in Chapter 2, can be of help in these cases. But the types of 'rules' that can be formulated would include:

- always use 'I' when a personal statement is being made, in order to claim ownership;
- unless you are referring to a number of people and their views and/or actions, do not use 'they';
- only use 'we' – for example, 'we decided at a particular stage...' – when in fact the decision was made by 'we' and not 'I';
- refer to people by name and when asking a particular person a question include their name in the question so that they are completely aware that it is them and not another person who is being asked the question;
- wherever possible, keep the situation to 'now', the 'here and now' of the interactive situation rather than a historical, futuristic or hypothetical event.

OTHER EXPERIENTIAL AND INTERACTIVE MODELS

The straightforward modification of behaviour as described above is not the only model approach for experiential activities in interactive learning. Every model has its followers who firmly believe that the model they support is the most effective. The choice is yours, but one piece of advice I can give is that the more complicated and complex the model, the more intervention it usually requires by the facilitator. You should read about, experience, experiment with and practise as many of the different approaches as you can – it is only in this way that you can determine the model with which you feel most comfortable. Any other will usually show that you are not happy with the approach and this will be readily transmitted to the learners, whether you intend it or not. Two recommended books that will describe methods, approaches, models and activities are by Rae (1985) and Burnard (1992).

References

Rae, Leslie (1985) *The Skills of Human Relations Training*, Gower.
Burnard, Philip (1992) *Interpersonal Skills Training*, Kogan Page (includes 110 activities suitable for interpersonal skills training).

13

Miscellaneous Activities and Closures

A number of activities that are used in training and development belong to no specific category of activity, but are useful within any training programme. Among these you can identify trust exercises, validation activities and closure activities. Closure activities can often be synonymous with the validation of a programme, but here validation will include only those activities that are different from the completion of validation and evaluation sheets.

TRUST EXERCISES

Description

Although this type of activity occurs most frequently in interpersonal learning programmes, it can be used in a variety of situations, including leadership and team development. It serves the purpose, after initial activities in a programme have moved the group along the path to awareness and the start of relationships, of reinforcing these relationships by increasing the mutual trust among the members. Trust is an essential element of most training and development programmes, especially in such learning events as outdoor training. Most trust activities are relatively simple, frequently physical and sometimes including an element of risk, although the latter should be kept to an absolute minimum by adherence to the safety standards required in outdoor training.

Membership and timing

It will be obvious that in a learning group everybody should take part in trust activities in order to develop relationships as widely as possible within the group. Time may not permit every learner to interact with every other learner, but every attempt should be made to cast the net as extensively as possible.

Timing can vary considerably, depending on the complexity of the activity, but usually each activity is relatively short, necessarily so because too much overt emphasis should not be placed on the event.

Preparation, design and usage

Most trust activities by virtue of their relative simplicity require little in the way of planning and design apart from the initial decisions to include them, where to include them in the programme and which activities to use. Written briefs are rarely necessary, introduction to the activity usually being a verbal briefing by the trainer, or in some cases a demonstration of what the learners will be asked to do.

However, the decision on whether to use a trust activity or not should not be taken lightly as there is frequently the chance of emotional risk. In the past, trust games have been played for reasons not always related to the needs of the learners and have gained a bad name in some circles. Many of the activities require physical touching, an act that not everybody is willing to accept, and no pressure should be applied for people to take part, nor even more than limited persuasion used where there is hesitation.

THE TRUST WALK

This is a commonly used trust activity which includes a range of learning in addition to the trust element. The learning group is paired off and one of each pair is blindfolded. The other person is instructed to take the blindfolded person for a walk – in the grounds of the training establishment, for example – the sighted person leading the other around obstacles, taking care that they are not hurt or placed in any danger. Constraints placed upon the pair can include a prohibition on any verbal comment in the form of movement instructions, although the pair can talk about anything else as they walk around. Usually pairs work out a non-verbal, tactile means of communicating such advice as where there is a step up or down, a requirement to stop and go and so on. During the walk the sighted person should watch out for objects that the blindfolded person can touch to determine by that sense alone the texture, feel, smell, even taste of the objects. These feelings can form part of the conversation as the trust walk proceeds. Another intervention on the part of the sighted person might be to stop the walk so that the other person can listen – to birds, animals, traffic, silence – and to test the air by the sense of smell.

At the end of about ten minutes, when the pair is at the furthest point from the training room, the roles are reversed and the pair returns to the training room, similar methods being used as on the outward part of the walk.

When all pairs have returned to the training room, usually after about a total half-hour interval, it is suggested that the pairs discuss the experience, describing such aspects as feelings, differences from a normal walk, the fact of blindness and the differences caused by this and the way that trust developed – if in fact it did! Following the paired discussion, the trainer can lead a full group discussion encouraging the general and significant learning points to emerge in a sharing manner.

This is an activity that can be used quite early in an event and my experience has been that it almost always accelerates trusting relationships within the group or team.

PHYSICAL TRUST

A number of other trust exercises exist that are based on the leading participant having sufficient trust in the others of the group to engage in physical activities in which they have to rely on the others not to allow them to be hurt.

Examples of this type of activity include:

- The participants stand in a circle with one member in the centre, either blindfolded or with eyes shut. The central person allows him or herself to fall backwards and be stopped from hitting the floor by a member in the circle. This is repeated several times, then another member takes the central position, and so on. Most people report that the first and second time they fall they are terrified because they seem to fall such a long way before being stopped, but the feeling of trust soon emerges.
- One person lies on the floor, with eyes shut, and is encouraged to relax their muscles and not resist. The other members, usually four or six people, place their hands under the prone member and lift them to waist, chest or even shoulder height, depending on the size and weight of the

prone member and the strength and size of the weakest member of the lifting group. Again, the exercise would be repeated with the other members of the group.

■ One with a little more physical risk is when six people face each other and hold the arms of their opposite number to form a cradle. A seventh person runs and dives on to the cradle. An eighth person might act as longstop at the end of the cradle, as an additional safety factor.

These and other physical trust games are all intended to develop mutual physical trust between the members of a group who are working or will work with each other. Physical trust, although giving no guarantee, will help in the movement towards other forms of trust, trust that will become necessary as the learning event develops.

You should ensure that all the members are aware of the objectives of the activities and the relevance to the learning programme, but even then you should be prepared for resistance on occasions or by some individuals. Often they fail to see the relevance, or feel the activities are 'silly games' – perhaps you have not been clear in stating the reasons and objectives if these are the reactions and you should reflect on how you have presented the activity. The most difficult situation is when most but not all of the group is willing to go ahead with trust activities, even when you have explained clearly the reasons for suggesting it. If you accept the wishes of one group, you run the danger of alienating the other and simply doing nothing does not help the progress of the group. One approach to this that I have used successfully is to let the willing ones go ahead with the activities, while the other group is given a task to perform – a suitable one I have found is for them to discuss and list the pros and cons of using trust games in specific types of learning programmes, for submission to the group that has taken part in the activities!

VALIDATION ACTIVITIES

Many of the approaches to validate and evaluate training programmes are part of a substantial and comprehensive scheme and instrumentation and I have written elsewhere about these (Rae, 1991).

Validation and evaluation of *activities* normally occur at the interim and end of programme stages. Interim validation is probably best approached by means of activities, in this way continuing the activities that have probably formed part of the learning to that stage; a more academic approach might be seen as a retrograde step by the learners.

Reviews can be of a minor nature or more substantial, taking a while to perform. Whichever approach is used there is at least one essential – do not ask the learners what they want from the event unless you are in a position to provide this, whether this means the injection of new material, a repetition of material that has obviously not been sufficiently clearly presented or a reinforcement of other material. All these take time, time for which you may not have planned, but which, if stated as required by the learners, must be given. If you are not in a position to do anything about the event failings, do not ask the question!

DIURNAL REVIEWS

The principle to observe concerning validation during a learning event is that overuse can get in the way of the learning and be resented by the learners. So the second axiom is only to seek views if it is essential that you become aware of the progress of the learning to that stage in the event and the information can only be obtained this way. Many longer programmes seek review of progress on a daily basis, or at the end of a specific section of learning material.

Two schools of thought exist about when to review. Basically you ask the learning group, perhaps in subgroups, to meet and discuss the event so far, what they have learned, what they have not learned because of some difficulty and any other comments they wish to make. They are then asked to present their views to you, perhaps accompanied by a flipchart sheet that can be posted and referred to later. There may be differences of opinion between the subgroups and a plenary discussion can then take place to resolve or collate these differences. You will need to take note of their requirements, if any, and take immediate steps to resolve the problems. This is the reason why you must ensure that if you ask the question you have time to deal with the answer.

The difference of opinion over these diurnal validation discussions is whether they should take place at the end of the training day or at the start of the next day. If they are held at the end of the day memory and views of what has happened are fresh in the mind of the learners, whereas if the review is delayed until the next morning it may be incomplete because of reduced recall and also a desire on the part of the learners to get on with the next aspects of the training. My personal preference is to review the following morning, linking this with a review of learning log that the learners will have completed the previous evening and which they will be presenting that morning. This also acts as an active start to the day, based on something about which they have comments. However, some trainers prefer the evening review, particularly if it is felt that all might not be well, and consequently they will have some time to prepare for the next day to try to resolve some of the problems.

INTERIM REVIEWS

There are innumerable interim review instruments, both traditional and more novel. My experience is that, unless scientific accuracy is required (which is rare and not always possible), novel approaches are appreciated by the participants and the required results are obtained without an over-serious instrument. One or two of these different approaches are described here, but there are many more that enable you to ring the changes.

THE 'BLOB' REVIEW

This is an instant form of progress review, and its immediateness and spontaneity may cause you problems if there are content aspects of the event that have to be dealt with or repeated. In addition, the review itself can take an hour or so, but this will be well worth it if you are unsure about how an event is progressing.

One common variation of this activity is to:

1. Ask each individual to write down three significant statements that they would like to make about the programme so far.
2. Divide the learning group into pairs to decide from the joint six statements they have brought to the meeting which three they wish to carry forward.
3. When the three statements have been decided upon, groups of four should be formed, with the similar brief of deciding on three statements from the six brought to the group.
4. If time and numbers permit, groups of eight can then be formed to decide on six statements to be the final agreed comments.
5. The six final statements should be entered on a chart similar to the one shown in Figure 13.1 and any clarification necessary made by the originators of the statement.

6. All the members should then come to the chart and place a blob – ● – in the column relating to the rating with which they agree. The columns can be headed 'SD' = strongly disagree; 'D' = disagree; 'A' = agree; 'SA' = strongly agree with the statement.

Once all the views have been entered, a pattern will emerge about the views of the learning group that will indicate if there are any problems that require immediate action.

Set of statements	SD	D	A	SA

Figure 13.1 *'Blob' validation chart*

THE TEMPERATURE GAUGE

This is a fun way of obtaining progressive comments from the learners about how they see the learning programme at intervals throughout the event. Figure 13.2 shows the graphic that is drawn on a flipchart sheet and displayed at the beginning of the event. In the example, the views of the learners about the event's atmosphere are sought, but a number of different views or feelings can be used instead. The learners are asked as individuals to come and make a personal mark (full initials, for example) at the 'temperature' they feel best represents how they view the programme. Any major divergences should be questioned, but no undue pressure should be put on a member to explain their views if they are reluctant to do so. Usually, at the next stage the divergent member(s) frequently volunteer to comment on their divergences if they still exist, or why they existed on the previous occasion.

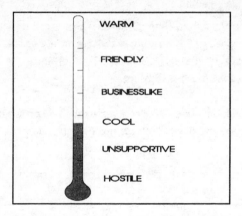

Figure 13.2 *The course atmosphere*

At some stage in the event (or stages depending on the length of the programme) and at the end ask the members to enter their marks in the same way. As a result the variations in the programme reception can be monitored, visibly for all to see, and any problems dealt with as they arise, or soon after. An effective time to have the diagram completed is immediately before the lunch break, rather than at the start or end of the day, or immediately after lunch!

HAPPY FACES

A variation of the thermometer is to have displayed on a chart a number of faces with the mouths in progressive stages from smiling broadly to scowling or looking very miserable, as shown in Figure 13.3.

The learners are asked to place a mark beside the face that best represents how they feel. Again this process can be repeated several times during the event to show the changes and identify problems that need to be resolved. Variations to the 'smiling' face can include the size of an open mouth to show how much the members feel they have the opportunity to participate.

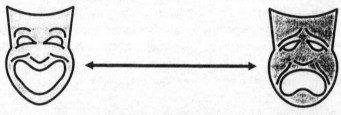

Figure 13.3 *Happy faces*

THE STEERING WHEEL

One of the uses of this graphic can be to enable the learners to show how they feel about the pace of the course, the steering wheel obviously reflecting a car and speed. Participants can enter their personal mark in the sector with which they identify, as in Figure 13.4.

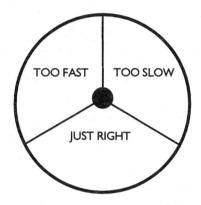

Figure 13.4 *The speed of the course*

END-OF-PROGRAMME REVIEWS

The usual review or validation at the end of a programme is through the use of a validation or reactionnaire questionnaire. If these are well-designed they can give you a considerable amount of valuable, objective information about the value of the training and the extent of the learning and can provide permanent records of this information. But less formal approaches can be used, including the final completion of one of the graphic approaches described above.

Otherwise, the programme review can be achieved by:

- a full group discussion review;
- buzz or subgroup reviews;
- poster identification.

The full group discussion review is usually led by the trainer with the full learning group in the same room. The discussion can be started by a question such as 'What views do you have on how the programme has gone?', but usually this is too general to produce rational and comprehensive responses. The group usually requires some help in identifying areas on which it can comment, and this help can be provided by the display of a flipchart on which are entered a number of subject areas on which the trainer would like comments. This chart can progress the discussion in a rational manner, using the chart as a visible 'shopping list'. Prescription of the areas for discussion must not be absolute and every opportunity should be given to the learners to comment on subjects that are not included in the list, and also to contribute as they wish to the final entry 'Any other comments?'

The problems with this approach, particularly if the group is larger than six or eight members, include:

- not everybody has the opportunity to speak;
- the quieter members can hide in the group and not contribute;
- the more active, reactive members can dominate the discussion and only their views emerge.

Many of these problems can be avoided to a large extent by the use of buzz or subgroups, when the learning group is divided into small groups of three people. The groups are given time to discuss the questions that have been posed, and to add their own comments, in the small group situation in which everybody has the chance to speak. At the end of the divided period the groups are brought back to the full group and spokespersons from each group present the views of their groups, using the control techniques described earlier in the book. A more general discussion can follow these presentations, divergences being clarified as they arise.

Poster identification

This approach avoids the traditional group discussion methods described above, and introduces a more graphic approach. Flipchart sheets are posted around the walls of the training room with pre-prepared statements or questions written on them. The learners are invited to go round the posters and add their comments, with their names if they wish. Alternatively, each participant can be given a number of Post-It stickers on which to write their comments and stick to the relevant chart. When all the comments have been made the learners are encouraged to wander round and read all the reviews, after which a summary review from the comments entered can be made, either with the trainer leading the review or the learners commenting on the areas that have interested them. Typical questions that can be entered on the sheets can include:

The part of the course that I liked most was...
The part of the course that I liked least was...
The part of the course that I hated was...
This course would have been better/more appropriate/more
    enjoyable for me if...
If I had to start this course again, I would...
If I had to start this course again, I would not...
When I first arrived I felt...
What would have made me feel better would have been...
My feelings at this moment in general terms are...
My feelings about the course at this moment are...
The main thing I have learned is...
What I have learned on the course and will make most use of at
    work is...

You may wish to experiment with the questions and types of questions you wish to pose for your particular training programmes, even to the extent of just having two sheets – one headed 'Good points about the programme', the other 'Bad (or less good) points about the programme' – or some number of sheets in between this and the list shown above.

CLOSING

Action planning

There are countless ways in which you can end a learning programme, apart from simply saying 'Thank you and goodbye!' An ideal approach is to ensure that the end of the course is not the end of the learning and that the learners continue developing when they return to work. The simplest form of this is an Action Plan that the learners complete before leaving the programme, take with them back to work, discuss with their boss and then implement. Simply said, but not so easily performed in practice. Your role as trainer is to start the operation, encourage them to continue with it and perhaps liaise with the line managers to ensure that they perform their action role.

Action Plans can be as complex as you and the learners wish, but the principle of 'the simpler it is, the more likely it will be actioned' should be borne in mind. The basic features of any action planning are:

- What are you going to do?
- When or by when are you going to do it?
- How are you going to do it?

These aspects are simple enough, but sufficiently comprehensive to ensure successful translation of the learning to work, the amount of detail being entered being left to the learners themselves. A typical Action Planning format can be as shown in Figure 13.5.

Planned action	When or by when	How I shall do it?
Action 1.		
Action 2.		
Action 3.		

Figure 13.5 *An action planning format*

You might suggest to the learners that they should think in terms of no more than three or four planned actions, at least for immediate implementation. More than this can become daunting when they return to work and think about implementation.

Other closure activities

The principal trap you can fall into at the end of a programme, particularly a highly successful one, is to try to prolong it. If the learning aspects have been completed, Action Planning has taken place and any validation measures taken, usually all the learners then want to do is to leave in whatever emotional state they are. However, sometimes these emotions are still very high and they will welcome something that will help them to return to normality. This is particularly so at the end of a behavioural programme in which relationships have been developed and feelings encouraged to emerge.

One method of releasing feelings is to use a variation of the poster approach described above, but using rather more general questions and statements. Such statements could include:

If I had to give a title to this course with the name of an animal, bird, insect, reptile, fish and so on, it would be...
If this course was a book, play or film, its title would be...
What I remember most about this group will be...
The most difficult part of the (period) for me was...
If I had to start working with this group again from the start, I would...
If I had to start working with this group again from the start, I would not...
Something I learned about other people was...
Something I learned about myself was...
Before we leave I would like you to tell me...
Before we leave I would like to tell you as a group...
Before we leave I would like to tell you (as many individuals as desired)...
Right now I am feeling...

Some variations of this may be the inclusion of you, the trainer, as after all you have been an integral part of the group for the period (it may be politic to confirm with the group that you can take part). Another variation, which would of course take rather longer, would be to invite the learning group to compose either their own statements or statements for the group activity.

The practical application of this again has a number of variations. One useful method is to give the learners a few minutes to compose their responses to the statements, then with the learners in a circle invite them all to present their responses in whatever order they wish. If some barriers still remain, the learning group can be invited to break up into pairs or threes and give their responses that are relevant in this grouping; then the full group comes together for the more group-related responses.

Individual feedback

As a final example of something to be used as a closure or farewell activity, sheets can be prepared with the name of each learner at the top. The sheets are distributed and each participant is invited to write a comment about the named learner, anonymously or with the commenter's name included. When all comments have been made, the sheets are given to the relevant person to take away with them as a memento of the event.

If you have any doubts that the comments will not all be positive and at least not be unkind, do not use this activity, as the good development achieved during the programme can be destroyed with even one un-kind comment, but this is not to say that you should only use this risky activity if everybody is going to be 'nice' to everybody else.

Whichever of these types of closure activities are used, have a good supply of tissues available!

Goodbye and good luck with your activities.

Reference

Rae, Leslie (1991) *How to Measure Training Effectiveness*, 2nd edn, Gower.

List of Activity Resources

The following list includes a selection of the resources currently available that are collections of activities of various kinds. It makes no pretence at being complete, although the number of collections listed should give any trainer or programme designer sufficient activities from which to choose for almost any type of programme. The list does not include those publications that are books with some activities included within the text. Nor does it include the vast range of structured activities published by Pfeiffer, USA (formerly University Associates).

Title	Author	Publisher	No of activities
20 Training Workshops for Customer Care, Vol 1	Gillen	Gower	20
20 Training Workshops for Customer Care, Vol 2	Cook	Gower	20
20 Training Workshops for Developing Managerial Effectiveness, Vols 1 and 2	Lewis, Kelly and Armstrong	Gower	40
25 Role Plays for Assertiveness Training	Bishop	Gower	25
25 Role Plays for Developing Counselling Skills	Couper and Stewart	Gower	25
25 Role Plays for Developing Management Skills	Kamp	Gower	25
25 Role Plays for Interview Training	Cox and Dufault	Gower	25
30 Training Sessions for Effective Presentation	Denham and Naylor	Gower	30
35 Ways to Start a Training Event	Rae	Fenman	35
50 Activities for Achieving Change	Fletcher	Gower	50
50 Activities on Creativity and Problem Solving	Cox, Dufault and Hopkins	Gower	50
50 Activities for Developing Counselling Skills	Bailey	Gower	50
50 Activities for Developing Management Skills, Vols 1 to 8	Various authors	Gower	400
50 Activities for Managing Stress	Bailey	Gower	50
50 Activities for Self-development	Francis and Woodcock	Gower	50
50 Problem Solving Activities	Badger and Chaston	Gower	50
50 Activities for Unblocking Organisational Communication, Vols 1 and 2	Francis	Gower	100

50 Activities for Unblocking your Organisation Vols 1 and 2	Francis and Woodcock	Gower	100
A Compendium of Icebreakers, Energizers and Introductions	Edited by Kirby	Gower	75
A Manual of Management Training Exercises	Payne	Gower	20
Activities for Achieving Managerial Effectiveness	Wilson	Connaught	35
Activities for Developing People Skills	Stewart and Couper	Connaught	50
Activities for Developing Supervisory Skills	Nicholls	Connaught	50
Activities for Trainers; 50 Useful Designs	Mill	University Associates	50
Customer Service Triggers	Kelly, Roger and Watson	Gower	40
Developing Cross-cultural Communication	Oomkes and Thomas	Connaught	70
Flexible Flipcharts	Richards	Fenman	50
Games for Trainers, Vols 1, 2 and 3	Kirby	Gower	225
Handbook of Management Games	Elgood	Gower	300
Icebreakers	Jones	Kogan Page	48
Imaginative Events, Vols 1 and 2	Jones	McGraw-Hill	48
Improving Work Groups: A Practical Manual for Team Building	Francis and Young	University Associates	46
Interpersonal Skills Training	Burnard	Kogan Page	110
Leadership Training	Christopher and Smith	Kogan Page	74
Meetings Management	Rae	McGraw-Hill	17
Presentation Skills	Fenwick	Fenman	20
Role Plays	Turner	Kogan Page	60
Role Plays for Interpersonal Skills	Williams	Connaught	25
Session Shakers	Cook	Fenman	50
Team Building	Parker and Kropp	Kogan Page	50
The Assertiveness Skills Pack	Gutman	Fenman	24
The Supervisor Development Pack	Fenwick	Fenman	15
The Trainer's Pocketbook of Ready to Use Exercises	Townsend	Mgt Pocketbooks	40
The Trainer's Quality Pack	Bray	Fenman	23
The Trainer's Toolkit	Melrose Mitchell	Melrose	17
Time Management Triggers	Kamp	Gower	35
Toolkit for Trainers	Pickles	Gower	60
Training for Assertiveness	Seifert	Gower	40
Training for Change	Bishop and Taylor	Kogan Page	50
Training for Time Management	Moon	Gower	22
Training Workshops for Supervisors	Atkinson and Feathers	Gower	5
Workshops that Work	Bourner, Martin and Race	McGraw-Hill	100

Total number of activities in this resource collection list = 3089

Appendix:
Choosing an Activity

The following is a checklist that you may wish to use when considering including an activity in your training programme.

- What are the learning objectives for your programme or part of the programme for which you are considering using an activity?
- What specifically should the learners have achieved by the end of the event?
- What is the existing level of knowledge or skill of the learners?
- What is the consequent learning gap that will be needed to be filled?
- Why do you want to use an activity?
- What advantages are there in using or not using an activity?
- To what extent will the activity fill the learning gap?
- Is time a relevant factor in your choice of an activity?
- How much time is available?
- To what extent have you activities available, knowledge of activities or know where to look for them?
- Can the activity you are considering be completed successfully in this time?
- Have you all the resources available to run the activity?
- What constraints – staffing, material resources, money, attitudes etc – exist?
- To what extent can you resolve the problems caused by these constraints?
- Have you considered what form of observation you want/need to use?
- Have you considered what form of review you want/need to use?

Index

Entries in *italics* refer to example activities described in the text.